'This close examination of current issues in African
bution to the debate within African institutions t
UN as it seeks to reflect in its practice a new level of understanding of the need for
strategic coherence with partnerships in Africa and elsewhere.'
**Ian Martin, executive director of Security Council Report, and member of the
UN High-Level Independent Panel on Peace Operations**

'The editors have assembled a highly qualified team of African analysts and practitioners
to shed considerable light on an important question: how effective is the emerging
"African model" of stabilization operations?'
Paul D. Williams, George Washington University

'From its outset the peacekeeping project has found its greatest challenges in Africa. This
collection, written for the most part by African researchers with frontline knowledge,
and offering clear and practical proposals, should be warmly welcomed by those in
positions to shape policy in Africa and beyond.'
Norrie MacQueen, University of St Andrews

'The contributors to this outstanding volume provide interesting views from a wide
angle on the future of peace operations in Africa. This book provides policy makers
and practitioners on the various political, security and humanitarian levels excellent
food for thought and discussion.'
**Maj Gen (ret) Patrick Cammaert, former military adviser and force commander,
UN Department of Peacekeeping Operations**

'A much-needed comprehensive overview of the emergence of an African model of
peace operations. It brings together leading African experts who offer a frank analysis
of recent developments in African security institutions and policy responses.'
Thierry Tardy, senior analyst, EU Institute for Security Studies

'With a formidable, multinational group of authors, this book charts the political,
policy and practical nuances of the task as Africans takes charge of building peace in
Africa. This is a very welcome and timely aid to our understanding of these issues.'
Dan Smith, director, Stockholm International Peace Research Institute

'An important book. It puts a much-needed focus on the changing nature and role of
African peace operations, and is a must-read for academics, practitioners and students
working with issues related to African security.'
Thomas Mandrup, Royal Danish Defence College and Stellenbosch University

'This book provides a rare combination of well-researched informative analysis with
clear policy recommendations. Clear and current, the book will be of use to practitioners, researchers and students. '
Jane Boulden, Queen's University Canada

Africa Now

Africa Now is published by Zed Books in association with the internationally respected Nordic Africa Institute. Featuring high-quality, cutting-edge research from leading academics, the series addresses the big issues confronting Africa today. Accessible but in-depth, and wide-ranging in its scope, *Africa Now* engages with the critical political, economic, sociological and development debates affecting the continent, shedding new light on pressing concerns.

Nordic Africa Institute

The Nordic Africa Institute (Nordiska Afrikainstitutet) is a centre for research, documentation and information on modern Africa. Based in Uppsala, Sweden, the Institute is dedicated to providing timely, critical and alternative research on and analysis of Africa and to co-operation with African researchers. As a hub and a meeting place for a growing field of research and analysis, the Institute strives to put knowledge of African issues within reach for scholars, policy-makers, politicians, the media, students and the general public. The Institute is financed jointly by the Nordic countries (Denmark, Finland, Iceland, Norway and Sweden).

www.nai.uu.se

Forthcoming titles

Anders Themnér (ed.), *Warlord Democrats in Africa*
Henning Melber (ed.), *The Rise of Africa's Middle Class*
Paul Higate (ed.), *Private Security in Africa*

Titles already published

Fantu Cheru and Cyril Obi (eds), *The Rise of China and India in Africa*
Ilda Lindell (ed.), *Africa's Informal Workers*
Iman Hashim and Dorte Thorsen, *Child Migration in Africa*
Prosper B. Matondi, Kjell Havnevik and Atakilte Beyene (eds), *Biofuels, Land Grabbing and Food Security in Africa*
Cyril Obi and Siri Aas Rustad (eds), *Oil and Insurgency in the Niger Delta*
Mats Utas (ed.), *African Conflicts and Informal Power*
Prosper B. Matondi, *Zimbabwe's Fast Track Land Reform*
Maria Eriksson Baaz and Maria Stern, *Sexual Violence as a Weapon of War?*
Fantu Cheru and Renu Modi (eds), *Agricultural Development and Food Security in Africa*
Amanda Hammar (ed.), *Displacement Economies in Africa*
Mary Njeri Kinyanjui, *Women and the Informal Economy in Urban Africa*
Liisa Laakso and Petri Hautaniemi (eds), *Diasporas, Development and Peacemaking in the Horn of Africa*
Margaret Lee, *Africa's World Trade*
Godwin R. Murunga, Duncan Okello and Anders Sjögren (eds), *Kenya: The Struggle for a New Constitutional Order*
Lisa Åkesson and Maria Eriksson Baaz (eds), *Africa's Return Migrants*
Thiven Reddy, *South Africa, Settler Colonialism and the Failures of Liberal Democracy*
Tobias Hagmann and Filip Reyntjens (eds), *Aid and Authoritarianism in Africa*

About the editors

Cedric de Coning is a senior researcher with the Peace Operations and Peacebuilding Research Group at the Norwegian Institute of International Affairs and a senior adviser on peacekeeping and peacebuilding for ACCORD.

Linnéa Gelot is a senior researcher at the Nordic Africa Institute in Uppsala, Sweden, a senior lecturer in peace and development studies at the School of Global Studies and an affiliated fellow of the Norwegian Institute of International Affairs.

John Karlsrud is senior research fellow and manager of the Training for Peace programme at the Norwegian Institute of International Affairs, working on peacekeeping, peacebuilding and humanitarian issues.

The future of African peace operations

From the Janjaweed to Boko Haram

edited by Cedric de Coning, Linnéa Gelot and John Karlsrud

Nordiska Afrikainstitutet
The Nordic Africa Institute

Zed Books
LONDON

The Future of African Peace Operations: From the Janjaweed to Boko Haram was first published in association with the Nordic Africa Institute, PO Box 1703, SE-751 47 Uppsala, Sweden in 2016 by Zed Books Ltd, The Foundry, 17 Oval Way, London SE11 5RR, UK.

www.zedbooks.co.uk
www.nai.uu.se

Typeset in Minion Pro by seagulls.net
Index: John Barker
Cover design: www.alice-marwick.co.uk

A catalogue record for this book is available from the British Library.

ISBN 978-1-78360-709-9 hb
ISBN 978-1-78360-708-2 pb
ISBN 978-1-78360-710-5 pdf
ISBN 978-1-78360-711-2 epub
ISBN 978-1-78360-712-9 mobi

Printed and bound by CPI Group (UK) Ltd, Croydon, CR0 4YY

Contents

Acknowledgements

The editors wish to thank the anonymous reviewers, as well as Ken Barlow and Dominic Fagan at Zed Books who helped bring this book project to fruition. We also gratefully recognize the support of the Nordic Africa Institute and the Norwegian-funded Training for Peace Programme.

This book is truly a collaborative effort, and many of the ideas herein originate from the seminar 'Strategic Options for the Future of African Peace Operations' in December 2014, held in Cape Town, South Africa. A very warm thank you to all the chapter contributors, it has been our pleasure to work together with you all.

We want to also especially acknowledge the help with tables, fact checks, and bibliography from Mr Sebastian Cavegård, intern at the Nordic Africa Institute and masters student in political science at Uppsala University.

Any remaining factual or linguistic errors remain our responsibility.

Acknowledgements

Abbreviations and acronyms

ACIRC	African Capacity for Immediate Response to Crises
ACOTA	Africa Contingency Operations Training Assistance
AFISMA	African-led International Support Mission to Mali
AMIS	African Union Mission in Sudan
AMISOM	African Union Mission in Somalia
APCs	armoured personnel carriers
APF	African Peace Facility
A-PREP	African Peacekeeping Rapid Response Partnership
APSA	African Peace and Security Architecture
ASEOWA	African Union support to Ebola Outbreak in West Africa
ASC	African Standby Capacity
ASF	African Standby Force
ASL	Ansar al-Sharia in Libya
AU	African Union
AUC	African Union Commission
CADSP	Common African Defence and Security Policy
CAR	Central African Republic
CEWARN	Conflict Early Warning and Response Mechanism
CEWS	Continental Early Warning System
CLB	Continental Logistics Base
COE	contingent-owned equipment
CPX	command post exercise
DPKO	Department of Peacekeeping Operations
DRC	Democratic Republic of the Congo
EASF	East African Standby Force
EASFCOM	East African Standby Force Coordination Mechanism
ECCAS	Economic Community of Central African States
ECOMOG	ECOWAS Ceasefire Monitoring Group
ECOWARN	ECOWAS Early Warning Network
ECOWAS	Economic Community of West African States
EDF	European Development Fund
EEAS	European External Action Service
ERM	Early Response Mechanism
EU	European Union
EVD	Ebola virus disease

FAO	Food and Agriculture Organization
FOC	full operational capability
FPUs	formed police units
FTX	field training exercise
IEDs	improvised explosive devices
IGAD	Intergovernmental Authority on Development
IGASOM	IGAD Peace Support Mission to Somalia
IOC	initial operational capability
IPOs	individually deployed police officers
LCBC	Lake Chad Basin Commission
LRA–RTF	Lord's Resistance Army–Regional Task Force
MAES	African Union's Operations in the Comoros
MICOPAX	ECCAS Mission for the Consolidation of Peace in the Central African Republic
MINUSMA	United Nations Multidimensional Integrated Stabilization Mission in Mali
MISAHEL	African Union Mission for Mali and the Sahel
MISCA	African-led International Support Mission to the Central African Republic
MNJTF	Multinational Joint Task Force
MNLA	National Movement for the Liberation of the Azawad
MONUSCO	United Nations Organization Stabilization Mission in the Democratic Republic of the Congo
MoU	Memorandum of Understanding
MSC	Military Staff Committee
MUJAO	Movement for Oneness and Jihad in West Africa
NARC	North African Regional Capability
NATO	North Atlantic Treaty Organization
OAU	Organization of African Unity
OCHA	UN Office for the Coordination of Humanitarian Affairs
PAE	Pacific Architects and Engineers
PCCs	police contributing countries
PLANELMs	planning elements
PSC	Peace and Security Council
PSSG	Police Strategic Support Group
PSOD	Peace Support Operations Division
QIPs	Quick Impact Projects
RDC	Rapid Deployment Capability
RECs	Regional Economic Communities
RLBs	Regional Logistics Bases
RMs	Regional Mechanisms

SADC	Southern African Development Community
SDF	Somali Defence Forces
STCDSS	Specialized Technical Committee of Ministers of Defence, Safety and Security
TAMs	technical assessment missions
TCCs	troop-contributing countries
TFG	Transitional Federal Government
TFIs	Transitional Federal Institutions
TOCs	transnational organized criminal activities
ToE	table of equipment
UNAMID	United Nations–African Union Mission in Darfur
UNISFA	United Nations Interim Security Force for Abyei
UNMEER	UN Mission for Ebola Emergency Response
UNOAU	United Nations Office to the African Union
UNSC	United Nations Security Council
UNSOA	United Nations Support Office to AMISOM
UNSOM	United Nations Assistance Mission in Somalia
USA	United States of America
WACD	West African Commission on Drugs
WAHO	West African Health Organization

1 | Towards an African model of peace operations

Cedric de Coning, Linnéa Gelot and John Karlsrud

Introduction

Highly complex and dynamic conflict systems are placing significant demands on African peace and security institutions. In response, new practices and cooperative models are emerging in an attempt to try to shape a more peaceful and stable continent. This book takes stock of how African peace operations have evolved over the past decade – from protecting internally displaced persons in Darfur from the Janjaweed militias to supporting coordinated operations by countries in the Lake Chad Basin region in their fight against Boko Haram insurgents. In the process we call for institutionalizing a new African peace operation model to better reflect the kind of short-duration, high-intensity, multi-actor stabilization operations that have become the norm.

African regional actors have during the last decade shown their indispensability as partners and as leading actors in international efforts to enhance peace and security in Africa (Brosig 2013; Engel and Porto 2014; Gelot 2012; Weiss and Welz 2014). The UN Security Council (UNSC) relies on proactive regional interventionism to sustain the reach and access of UN agencies to violence-affected populations in Africa as well as to prepare the ground for a transition to comprehensive UN-led peace operations. To this effect, the UNSC commends the growing role of the African Union (AU) in peace and security in its region and stresses the need for a stronger and more cohesive partnership between the UN and the AU in conflict prevention and resolution, rapid response to emerging crises, protection of children and peacebuilding (UNSC 2014; Boutellis and Williams 2013). While the UNSC in the 2005–10 period stressed the role of regional organizations, especially the AU, in responding to mass atrocities (UNSC 2006), the UNSC and the 'P3' – the United Kingdom, the United States and France – have since 2010 more actively aligned around the objective of closer cooperation with African regional actors to enable rapid reaction to counter contemporary regional and global security threats, among them criminal and terrorist networks, piracy, human trafficking and radicalized, armed non-state actors (UNSC 2014, 2015).

From experiences to date, a pattern of complex hybridity emerges. On the one hand, the UNSC relies on the AU and the Regional Economic Communities/

Regional Mechanisms (RECs/RMs) to act as first responders to emerging crises, and employ a generous interpretation of Chapter VIII of the UN Charter. An enduring trend in this regard is the UN's inability to generate troops and police in sufficient numbers and to deploy them rapidly enough to meet the demands made on it. Structural constraints, for example bureaucratic rationales and security and safety rules, as well as normative constraints, including the UN's core principles regarding impartiality, consent of all parties to the conflict, and non-use of force except in self-defence and in the defence of the mandate, have also resulted in a cautious posture. On the other hand, African regional actors rely on the UNSC's legitimacy for their actions and on financial and other types of assistance from international partners as well as African states and institutions, without which the African peace operations to date could not have occurred (Gelot 2012; Badmus 2015). African institutions are also developing and institutionalizing their peace and security mechanisms concurrently with peace operations being deployed, tested and assessed, given the complex conflict scenarios on the continent (De Coning 2014). Additionally, African institutions have ever closer and more complex relations with a multitude of actors – creating new relations of opportunity and dependency. Bilateral relations with conventional as well as new partners such as China and Russia, relations with diverse funding bodies, private sector partnerships, civil

---

Box 1.1 Background on the African Union and its peace and security architecture

The African Union (AU) was established in 2002 to reorganize and revitalize the Organization for African Unity (OAU), which was founded in 1963. While the OAU was based on principles of national liberation and decolonization, the AU is founded on principles of accelerated political and socio-economic integration between the Union's member states and its geographical regions. The transition from the OAU to the AU was made to envision an African future characterized by integration, prosperity and peace, which would be driven by the African people in order to become an influential voice within the international community (African Union Commission 2015: 10). In the peace and security realm the transition from the OAU to the AU broadened the security concept from state security to human security. One of the most significant shifts in this regard is the shift from non-interference (OAU) to non-indifference (AU) in that the Peace and Security Protocol of the AU provides for AU intervention in member states in cases of mass atrocities, war crimes and crimes against humanity.

At the core of the AU is the Assembly, made up by the heads of state from all fifty-four AU members, which is the highest level of decision-making within the Union (ibid.: 14). The Assembly can delegate tasks to either its Executive Council, which coordinates and monitors the implementation of adopted policies by the Assembly (ibid.: 22),

society participation, etc., are all necessary albeit accompanied by problematic challenges such as inter-institutional rivalry, incoherence and unaccountability (Tardy and Wyss 2014).

The emerging ASF is illustrative of a key component of the APSA that is simultaneously being refined, constructed and evaluated. This volume grapples with the realization that the doctrine of the ASF is out of sync with the challenges faced by African peace operations on the ground. The foundations for the ASF were laid over a decade ago. The existing doctrine has been developed around traditional principles of multidimensional UN peace operations. It will now have to adapt so that the ASF can deploy in high-intensity 'non-permissive' situations that the UN peace operation model was not originally designed for. Working assumptions and principles are in the process of being reconsidered, while the revised deadline for full operational capability (FOC) has remained the same, set for December 2015.[1]

As reflected in this volume in the chapters by Solomon Dersso and Jide Okeke (Chapters 3 and 7), the key question is how best to develop the Rapid Deployment Capability (RDC) concept, i.e. a process-based debate, and not how to, strictly speaking, operationalize the ASF on time. From recent discussion in the UNSC it is clear that the Western powers as well as emerging powers see a strategic value in supporting the development of an African rapid response

or its Peace and Security Council (PSC), which is mandated to decide on interventions in or sanctions against member states in order to prevent, manage and resolve conflicts within Africa. The African Peace and Security Architecture (APSA) includes the Continental Early Warning System (CEWS), the Panel of the Wise, the African Standby Force (ASF), the Military Committee and the Peace Fund.

The Permanent Representatives Committee (PRC) supports both the Assembly and the Executive Council (ibid.: 28) and is responsible for the day-to-day business, together with the AU Commission (AUC). The AUC functions as the AU's secretariat with approximately 1400 staff members managing the various AU programmes and initiatives in coordination with all of the different AU bodies (ibid.: 62).

Having individually developed outside of the AU/OAU structure, the Regional Economic Communities (RECs) are geographical groupings created to facilitate economic integration across the African continent. There are eight separate RECs which are recognized by and closely integrated with the AU: the Arab Maghreb Union (UMA), the Common Market for Eastern and Southern Africa, the Community of Sahel-Saharan States (CEN-SAD), the East African Community (EAC), the Economic Community of Central African States (ECCAS), the Economic Community of West African States (ECOWAS), the Intergovernmental Authority on Development (IGAD), and the Southern African Development Community (SADC) (ibid.: 116).

Adapted from African Union Commission (2015)

capability (African Union 2015a). It is widely recognized that Africa will need an RDC to mitigate the worst effects of erupting conflicts and to bridge the time it takes the APSA and other international actors to discuss strategic objectives and to plan and deploy more comprehensive missions (Badmus 2015).

Against the background of the gap between current conflict scenarios and the ASF concept, Dersso and Okeke discuss one such proposal and its ambiguous standing within the APSA today, the 'African Capacity for Immediate Response to Crises' (ACIRC). Now considered an interim measure, supported by around fifteen African states, the ACIRC comprises tactical battle groups of 1,500 military personnel deployed by a lead nation or a group of AU member states. Volunteer states/coalitions would pledge to sustain troops in the field for a minimum of thirty days. Its purpose is to conduct stabilization and enforcement missions, neutralize terrorist groups, and provide emergency assistance to AU member states. Unlike the ASF regional standby forces, the ACIRC is a purely military capability without police or civilian elements. Rapid reaction and stabilization demands have taken centre stage, reflecting a sense of urgency within the APSA communities, against the backdrop of complex crises in Mali, Central African Republic (CAR) and elsewhere.

In this volume, chapters discuss the factors that led to an emergent hybrid global–regional partnership in peace and security matters against the background of global order change. We discuss how the perceptions of a changed security landscape and the related perception of an urgent need to act have sparked processes of adaptation and response within an evolving APSA. Sometimes the chapters treat the AU or the RECs/RMs as coherent actors, yet in keeping with recent scholarship on the APSA (Brosig 2013; Engel and Porto 2014; Tardy and Wyss 2014; Badmus 2015) the intense overlap and institutional relations between institutions and policy communities as well as the various and changing interests within the components of the APSA and between the APSA and the member states are also recognized. For instance, de Coning argues (Chapter 9) that most of the AU peace operations to date are better understood as coalitions of the willing, rather than as multinational-led and -deployed operations as foreseen in the ASF.

A theme that also underpins the chapters is the ways in which subregional organizations negotiate political autonomy and craft for themselves a distinct profile or niche competence. Regularly, the APSA becomes an institutional setting for subregional actors and state leaders to join forces and contest the argument that outside/global actors should interfere with sovereignty and local politics. Facing transnational security challenges, the RECs/RMs need close inter-institutional linkages with the APSA to strengthen the joint capacity to respond. Yet within their own subregions institutions and regional states claim first-response authority. There are thus processes of convergence and alignment as well as divergence or friction.

The APSA provides institutional space for African states and policy-makers to make the collective case at the global level that African regional powers and institutions are providing regional security goods and thus shouldering international responsibilities. Following on from that, they argue that growing influence on international security should translate into recognition and representation in global governance fora (Wallensteen and Bjurner 2015). The chapters also grapple with the implications of the APSA's financial dependency on external funding and discuss initiatives to increase African internal sources of funding. The literature on African security has consistently argued that dependency on financial assistance challenges the principle of ownership (De Coning 1997; Boutellis and Williams 2013), and even that on occasion a funding institution or partner may appear as an actor of equal significance to the APSA on matters of peace and security (Brosig 2013).[2]

The context: the contemporary African security landscape

African peace operations, in collaboration with international partners, are responding to a highly complex and dynamic environment. To meet rapidly changing conflict patterns and security trends, a rich variety of institutional interlinkages and hybrid partnership models have emerged, but these models are often poorly developed or institutionalized. There is a need to develop both resilient African models and collaborative approaches.

As Kwesi Aning and Mustapha Abdallah (Chapter 2) highlight, asymmetric and hybrid security challenges, religious extremism and transnational criminal networks intersect in several countries, creating new challenges for the APSA and resulting in calls for rapid action. Thanks to intensive efforts, piracy off the Horn of Africa has waned – but is on the rise in other areas such as the Gulf of Guinea. Militant groups and jihadist terrorist networks are changing their modus operandi; and in some areas, collusion between criminal or militant actors, business actors and state structures brings additional challenges. However, while religious extremism and terrorism are important factors, they should not be overemphasized or allowed to mask deeper political and socio-economic challenges that are at risk of becoming 'securitized'.[3]

Pandemics such as Ebola, as Aning and Abdallah also note, pose immense challenges to areas with weak state authority or widespread poverty. With the Ebola pandemic in West Africa as an example, discussion has begun on whether rapid intervention may be needed also in cases of instability or pandemics, and not only in extreme cases of mass atrocities and crimes against humanity. The most extreme cases are covered under Article 4(h) of the AU Constitutive Act and may trigger military intervention by the AU on a member state's territory, even finally without its consent (Engel and Porto 2013).

Complex intercommunal conflicts with regional and transnational dimensions pose threats to the protection of civilian populations and require careful responses by African institutions. At the same time, prefixes such as 'asymmetric' or 'novel' applied to threats mask the fact that conventional threats to security continue to exist in parallel with unpredictable and fragmented actors and drivers of conflict.

The transformation of peace and security institutions in response to contemporary security challenges is a broader transnational debate, and it is worthwhile to reflect on the parallel debates regarding stabilization within the UNSC and UN Department of Peacekeeping Operations (DPKO) as well as some pivotal UN member states (De Coning 2015). UN peace operations are evolving in the direction of more 'robust war-fighting mandates', and in the academic literature there is a discussion of implications for long-term political stability and for UN peace operations to serve UN Charter principles (Berdal and Ucko 2015; Karlsrud 2015). In the post-Cold War period, the expectations for the UNSC to engage in civil wars to restore state authority and to protect civilians, even in the absence of a UN-mediated political process, have led to persistent calls for changed political principles, enabling arrangements and capabilities (UNSC 2013; UN 2015).

However, as Berdal and Ucko note (2015: 8), the more volatile the environments are, the harder it has become for the UN to generate well-equipped troops and police units and specialized capabilities. In regard to Africa, Western militaries prefer to deploy their troops and police unilaterally, under coalitions of the willing arrangements or alternatively under the EU or NATO flag, entering into ad hoc relations with African institutions. In one example, unilateral actions by France in Mali successfully contained Islamist militants in the north of the country in 2013/14. In fact, as Okeke and De Coning discuss (Chapters 7 and 9), frustrations with the French intervention in Mali stimulated a debate within the AU about the inadequacies of the ASF and this led to the ACIRC being proposed. Delimited and short-duration missions such as France's in Mali are not often linked to or supportive of a long-term political objective (Berdal and Ucko 2015: 9–10).

In addition, notwithstanding the trend towards hybrid multi-actor peace operations, delimited stabilization missions of this kind are not usually from the start well linked to regional political dynamics. One negative implication, among many possible, as shown in Mali, is that the Economic Community of West African States (ECOWAS) and UN follow-on forces (MINUSMA) came under attack once the French force withdrew. Hybrid peace operation developments thus come with advantages – for example, flexibility and speed – but they have some problematic implications. Dominant or interested states can 'play a multilateral game' through cooperative and hybrid arrangements with a UN mandate while at the same time retain political independence in strategic decisions, and perhaps also test and explore new directions in military doctrine (Karlsrud 2015; Tardy 2014).

Hence, the traditional model of multidimensional UN peacekeeping has been eroded and is no longer the one we see deployed in some of today's complex crises. It has been asked whether the mandates for the peacekeeping missions in the CAR (MINUSCA), DRC (MONUSCO) and Mali (MINUSMA) herald a change in UN peacekeeping culture towards stabilization and peace enforcement missions and what the effects will be for the UN's foundational principles of impartiality, consent and non-use of force except in self-defence and in defence of the mandate (Karlsrud 2015).

Drivers behind an African shift towards stabilization operations can be said to be normative, geopolitical and historical/empirical. The APSA was founded with a normative objective in mind: to enable African peace and security structures to respond to armed conflicts and human rights abuses, and to be conceptually and materially equipped to take robust action when needed to protect civilians (Engel and Porto 2013) Through the institutional setting of the APSA, African regional powers as well as influential policy-makers also pursue strategic interests within a changing global order. A niche role in peace and security, building on the comparative advantages of regional actors, thus forms part of a strategic narrative to enhance the influence of African states and institutions in global governance.

Empirically, a dominant perception is that new security threats are emerging and that these pose previously unknown risks to communities, peacekeepers and institutions (Tardy and Wyss 2014). Stabilization has become seen as necessary to embark on restoration of state authority and comprehensive protection-of-civilians measures. The move towards increasingly comprehensive and complex African peace operations, in turn, is justified by the experiences to date (Badmus 2015). In just the last ten years, the AU and the RECs/RMs have fielded over ten peace operations to Burundi, the CAR, Comoros, Darfur, Mali and Somalia. In 2013 alone, a total of approximately 40,000 uniformed and civilian personnel were mandated to serve in AU peace operations (approximately 71,000, if the joint African Union–United Nations (UN) hybrid mission in Darfur is also taken into account) (Lotze 2013). Throughout 2014 and in early 2015 this number was around 30,000 personnel.

As a result of these developments, the AU and the RECs/RMs have had to respond to increasingly complex security environments over the last decade. Has this resulted in the emergence of an African model of peace operations? If so, how could we characterize such an African model? And how should African member states respond to situations that increasingly cross the boundaries between their countries and their regional contexts where there are active RECs/RMs?

Mission	Leading institution	Mandate
Economic Community Ceasefire Monitoring Group (ECOMOG), Liberia	ECOWAS	Supervise implementation of and compliance with ceasefire agreement
African Union Mission in Burundi (AMIB)	AU	Supervise, observe, monitor and verify implementation of ceasefire agreement
Economic Community Mission in Liberia (ECOMIL)	ECOWAS	Monitor and establish successful disengagement and disarmament of armed factions
African Union Mission in Sudan (AMIS)	AU	Contribute to general security; delivery of humanitarian relief in Darfur; monitoring cease fire and peace agreements
African Union Mission for Support to the Elections in Comoros (AMISEC)	AU	Provide secure environment for the 2006 elections in Comoros
African Union Mission in Somalia (AMISOM)	AU	To support dialogue and reconciliation in Somalia; protection for federal institutions and civilians; security for key infrastructure
African Union Electoral and Security Assistance Mission to the Comoros (MAES)/Operation Democracy	AU	Support secure environment and monitoring of election process
United Nations–African Union Mission in Darfur (UNAMID)	AU/UN	Contribute to general security and humanitarian relief
Regional Task Force of the African Union-led Regional Cooperation Initiative for the Elimination of the Lord's Resistance Army (RCI-LRA)	AU	Conduct counter-LRA operations and protect civilians
African-led International Support Mission to Mali (AFISMA)	AU/ECOWAS	Support restoration of state authority and protect civilians
African-led International Support Mission to the Central African Republic (MISCA)	AU/ECCAS	Support restoration of state authority and protect civilians
Multinational Joint Task Force (MNJTF) of the Lake Chad Basin Commission against Boko Haram	LCBC	Conduct operations aimed at preventing the expansion of Boko Haram

Table 1.1 African peace operations, 1990–2015

Strategic partners	Duration	Authorized troop strength, police and civilian components
UN, United States	August 1990–June 1999	Approximately 3,500 uniformed personnel
UN	April 2003–June 2004	Approximately 3,500 uniformed personnel
UN, United States	September 2003–October 2003	Approximately 3,600 uniformed personnel
EU, UN	October 2004–December 2007	Approximately 3,320 authorized personnel, including 2,341 uniformed, 815 police and some civilians
EU, UN	21 March 2006–9 June 2006	462 uniformed personnel, police and civilians
EU, UN	January 2007–	Approximately 22,126 uniformed personnel
EU	May 2007–October 2008	Approximately 160 uniformed personnel
None	July 2007–	Approximately 19,555 uniformed personnel and 6,432 police
EU, United States	March 2012–	Approximately 5,000 uniformed personnel
EU, UN	December 2012–July 2013	Approximately 9,620 uniformed personnel and 171 civilians
EU, France, UN	December 2013–September 2014	Approximately 2,475 uniformed personnel, 1,025 police and 152 civilians
AU	29 January 2015–	Approximately 8,700 uniformed personnel

Towards an African model of peace operations

Based on the contributions from the authors in this book, we argue that from the experiences of the AU and the subregions over the last decade, an *African model of peace operations* is emerging that is at odds with the mission scenarios and multidimensional assumptions that underpinned the original framework of the ASF. We find it useful to speak of an African model to assemble the key characteristics and the current possibilities and challenges that such operations represent for the continent.[4] The evolving model is one which relies on complex hybridity and mutual dependencies that transcend and problematize neat categories such as regional/global, top/down and dependency/ownership.

The African model of peace operations represents several implications for critical areas relevant to peace operations. The ASF will have to be revised and its RDC concept will have to adapt to changing challenges and conflict patterns. The AU and its partners will need to rethink their strategic considerations regarding the principle of subsidiarity, UN Charter Chapter VIII issues and the relationship between the UN, the EU, the AU and the RECs/RMs; the challenges and opportunities related to the mission support dimension of partnerships; doctrine, preparation and training of personnel and troops; and the development of the police and civilian dimension of African peace operations, as these capacities are of particular importance to achieve longer-term stability and facilitate the exit of African peace operations and/or transition to UN missions.

The African model of peace operations indicates that the AU has used its peace operations to contain violent conflicts, to protect governments and their citizens against aggressors and to help stabilize the security situation in the affected countries. Simultaneously, the AU has used its special envoys and good-offices mechanisms to seek lasting political solutions. The peace operations should not be seen in isolation as military solutions, but rather as part of a larger political intervention where the role of the peace operations is to contain violence and generate stability so that political solutions can be pursued (African Union 2015b). All the AU operations to date have been deployed amid ongoing conflict with the aim of halting the conflict and stabilizing the security situation. A fragile peace needs to be enforced by suppressing the capability of aggressors to use force for political purposes. The AU deploys 'stabilization operations', a term that we define, for the purposes of this volume, as: 'operations aimed at helping states in crisis to restore order and stability in the absence of a peace agreement, by using force and other means to help local authorities to contain aggressors (as identified in the relevant UNSC resolution), enforce law and order and protect civilians, in the context of a larger process that seeks a lasting political solution to the crisis'.

The AU will need to define and enhance conceptual clarity over the term 'stabilization', which has been quite contentious in policy as well as practice (see, e.g., Bachmann 2014). Internally, that will help in defining strategy and doctrine and in planning for upcoming roles.

During deployments, AU troops can act offensively and require intelligence capabilities, as well as the ability to implement stealth operations. Often, the only countries that are willing to contribute troops to such missions are those with regimes that have a strategic interest in securing the stability of the country in question, its neighbours and the subregion. The actual AU stabiliza-tion missions' experience has thus, at many levels, differed significantly from the UN peacekeeping model on which the ASF concept has largely been founded. Solomon Dersso (Chapter 3) reflects on this dilemma in his chapter and points to the discrepancies between all-encompassing mandates and limited availability of resources. He also highlights the continued dominance of military approaches, and the need for more focus on police and civilian dimensions to be able to undertake stabilization operations.

The interim rapid intervention proposal, the ACIRC, has been criticized for diverting attention from the operationalization of the ASF, while others consider that it has breathed new life into the RDC. We argue that it is important to revise the ASF while at the same time harmonizing a rapid deployment capacity within it to ensure that all African peace operations are brought into a multilateralist and international legal fold. In his chapter, Jide Okeke (Chapter 7) unpacks the relationship between the ACIRC and the ASF, and notes that while initially there was substantial tension, these instruments are now in a process of harmonization with the potential of speeding up the implementation of the ASF. He also points to the military focus and character of the ACIRC and therefore the perception among some that the ACIRC proposal indicated a militarization trend in African peace and security affairs. Additionally, he points to the need to update concepts to enable comprehensive and multidimensional stabilization missions on the continent, including vital police and civilian components. Another important point Okeke raises is the flexibility of the ASF – for example, in the war against Boko Haram the Lake Chad Basin Commission (LCBC) served as a temporary operational headquarters with ECOWAS being a temporary strategic headquarters for the Multinational Joint Taskforce (MNJTF) composed of troops from Benin, Cameroon, Chad, Niger and Nigeria. This shows that although the RECs/RMs are key constitutive parts of the ASF, the AU–REC/RM relationship can and must also embrace flexible solutions adjusted to specific security challenges that cross their boundaries and lines of authority.

African peace operations have so far predominantly been short-duration missions that are handed over to UN missions as soon as basic stability has been restored. All these African operations have subsequently been taken over by UN peace operations within six to eighteen months, except for the AU operation in Somalia.

In Somalia, the AU has had to fight an intensive and sustained counter-insurgency campaign to dislodge al-Shabaab. Despite considerable gains, the conditions have not been ripe yet for a UN mission to take over. As an exception and in recognition of the international and global significance of the work carried out by the AU, the UN Security Council has authorized the use of its assessed contributions to support the AU mission.

This characteristic of short-duration missions makes joint planning, analysis and preparedness for handover central issues from the very start. However, while a handover to the UN is the most plausible route, it is not guaranteed, so African missions should still be planned to be as distinct and 'minimally integrated' as possible. A UN takeover must not become the overriding objective of the operation since the case-specific political objectives in themselves are and should be primary. Therefore, the political objective and peacebuilding process need to be considered at the planning stage, taking into account the vital role of civilians and police.

While the trend of handing over African missions to the UN is likely to continue, Yvonne Akpasom argues (Chapter 8) that future African missions should be expected to include a civilian dimension to start facilitating the restoration of state authority and state–society relations in newly liberated areas to keep the fragile peace from breaking apart again. Future African missions are likely to continue to be robust in nature and must include a civilian casualty tracking cell such as that developed for AMISOM, as well as other instruments that help to minimize harm against civilians.

As these missions are funded and supported by the international community, the AU and the RECs/RMs cannot independently take decisions on the mandate, size and duration of these missions (De Coning 1997). A key question is what must be done to incentivize African countries to support an institutionalized force for peace operations, funded and sustained by African states themselves? Both the ACIRC and the ASF are African initiatives to institutionalize capacities to respond more rapidly to sudden-onset crisis. However, the ASF has been overly dependent on partner support. In response to increased pressure on African states to take up more of the burden for funding African peace operations, both from within Africa and from partners, the June 2015 AU summit decided that African member states should contribute at least 25 per cent of the cost of AU peace operations. In 2015, that would mean approximately US$250 million, and if it had been immediately implemented it would have resulted in a 50 per cent increase in the annual budget of the AU. Such a radical increase was found to be unrealistic and it was decided that this new scale of assessment will be gradually introduced over the next five years. It remains to be seen whether these pledges made by African member states will materialize, and what consequences this will have for the global partnership on peace operations. If African member states take on a reasonable share of the burden, the AU's partners are more likely to consider a predictable funding model for AU operations. The lack of predictable funding and support to date has meant that AU missions have had to make do with fewer personnel and resources than a UN mission would have had in the same theatre. For instance, in Darfur the UN mission that followed on from AMIS had approximately three times as many personnel and four times the budget. The same trend can be observed in the UN missions that followed on from the AU missions in Mali and the CAR.

There have been other serious attempts to consider alternative ways of funding the AU. A team of experts led by former Nigerian president Obasanjo has proposed various ways in which the AU can raise its own funding. For instance, a levy of US$10 on plane tickets to Africa and US$2 on hotel accommodation could raise more than US$700 million annually (African Union 2014b). These measures have not yet been adopted, but they serve as examples that it is not impossible for the AU to generate types of alternative funding. The steady rise in the defence budgets of many African member states, with a 65 per cent average increase over the last decade (Perlo-Freeman and Solmirano 2014), inadvertently indicates a growing ability to fund and support collective security mechanisms, including African peace operations.

African peace operations: partnerships and support

Given the highly transnationalized intervention 'space', the subsidiarity principle needs further discussion and clarification, as Michelle Ndiaye's (Chapter 4) analysis of the perspectives on this concept of the AU and the RECs/RMs respectively makes clear. African peace operations that entail the use of force require UNSC mandates under Chapter VII of the UN Charter. Moreover, judging from experiences to date, the deployment of African peace operations requires the further authorization of the AU PSC. If a REC/RM is mobilized to undertake such an operation, authorization may also be necessary from the REC/RM's own legal authorizing body. For other mission types that do not require legal authority to use force, the body most proximate – the relevant REC/RM – should be assumed to have responsibility for responding first.

In her chapter on the principle of subsidiarity Michelle Ndiaye offers an insightful analysis of the balance that must be struck between, on the one hand, the political will and operational competence that subregional organizations often are able to muster and, on the other, the legal authority and political legitimacy that the AU and UNSC provide. She finds that all actors responding to a conflict need to ensure close and regular communication to enable assessments of comparative advantage, deployed capabilities and available resources, as well as efficiency and legitimacy. As seen from the discussions around which organization should have the main authority for the mission in Mali, personal relationships, fast-paced regional dynamics and rapid adaptation have been key to understanding outcomes. However, the transition in the CAR and the current operation against Boko Haram suggest that some progress has been made in terms of cooperation between the RECs/RMs, the AU and other partners.

Moving on to investigate how the relationships between these organizations, as well as other stakeholders, have developed, Linda Darkwa (Chapter 5) details how the paradigmatic shift from the principle of non-interference to the principle of non-indifference and sovereignty as responsibility has precipitated the increased involvement by the AU and the RECs/RMs in maintaining African peace and security since the beginning of the millennium. In this endeavour, African peace operations have been mandated and deployed alongside various examples of subregional, UN or EU political/humanitarian/development presence. This creates challenges of duplication, overlap and rivalry, but also provides the AU, subregions, the EU and the UN with opportunities to collaborate, to coordinate their roles and to enter into burden-sharing arrangements and strategic partnerships. Darkwa drills deeper into what these strategic partnerships entail in terms of shared values and needs, and the ability to deliver to cover these needs. She emphasizes the requirement for a better articulation of the needs of the continent in a continental and cohesive strategy. This would enable the development of a more cohesive approach to peace and security partnerships and stabilization operations.

African peace operations are funded and supported in part by the AU, African troop- and police-contributing countries (TCCs, PCCs) and, in the case of the Ebola mission (ASEOWA), also by African private sector donations. Some subregions, such as the Economic Community of West Africa (ECOWAS), have been able to support their own missions through community levies. The MNJTF operation against Boko Haram is an example of an African operation that has been mostly self-funded. For instance, while the United States has contributed approximately US$5 million towards the campaign against Boko Haram in Nigeria, Nigeria itself has committed approximately US$100 million (World Affairs Journal 2015). However, AU peace operations remain dependent on funding and support from international organizations and partners for a large portion of their costs. In this regard, Darkwa connects the strength of the existing strategic partnerships with the pressing need to establish more predictable and effective means of funding, including from African member states and regions.

The Common African Position on the UN High-level Panel on UN Peace Operations called for a fresh look at the so-called Prodi proposal from 2008, which suggested using UN assessed contributions on a case-by-case basis to fund UNSC-authorized African peace operations, including the costs associated with deployed uniformed personnel (African Union 2015b). The report of the High-level Panel endorsed the African position and recommended such use

14

of UN assessed contributions, as a complement to funding from the AU and/ or African member states. It argued that it is in the UN's interest to help find predictable funding for AU operations, while, at the same time, it called on African states to take up more of the burden. The AU PSC subsequently welcomed the report of the UN High-level Panel, and agreed with the Panel that strategic and principled partnerships with regional organizations enable optimal use of their respective comparative advantages (African Union 2015c; UN 2015: 62–5). In its report the Panel observes that the United Nations 'today sits at the nexus of a loose web of international, regional and national capacities', and it calls for a stronger global–regional partnership (ibid.: 13). The Panel notes that interlocking and hybrid approaches amount to strategic networks that simultaneously allow for regional niche capacities (for instance, an 'African' model), flexibility and adaptability.

Mission support is critical to the success of African peace operations, but there has been insufficient investment in planning and management of missions. Walter Lotze (Chapter 6) argues that there continues to be a lack of predictability for mission support in his chapter, where he discerns four alternative models that have emerged to date. None of these actually responds to the dynamic and high-intensity environment that African peace operations are faced with. Flexible ad hoc models are often developed in response to specific contexts. Because of over-reliance on external support, there has been scant incentive to draft sufficient support models at the AU. The ad hoc approach is sometimes desirable and will in all likelihood continue, but there should be joint efforts at better planning and implementing support solutions, given the specific nature of African high-intensity peace operations. Although the models to be developed for future missions will be significantly influenced by the political will of partners, both the AU and the UN can identify what has worked and where improvements can be made. On a positive note, Lotze identifies increasing will among African member states to fund African peace operations, for example by providing US$50 million for AFISMA in Mali, and also the increased will to invest in training and equipping African troops in the CAR prior to the transition to a UN mission.

Several of the authors highlight the key role that civilians and police play in African peace operations, and the need to further strengthen their involvement to ensure the success of the missions. In her chapter, Yvonne Akpasom asserts that multidimensionality is a *sine qua non* for successful engagement in and support to countries emerging from conflict. She argues that the roles of civilians in mission planning at the AU PSOD should be reinforced, and more civilian planning capacity should be added at the strategic, operational and tactical levels of African peace operations. Planners must keep in mind the distinct nature of civilian roles in African peace operations – for instance, the particularities of police functions in stabilization contexts.

The AU needs to continue to develop the doctrinal framework and provide accepted guidelines on key concepts such as protection of civilians, gender, humanitarian support, and sexual exploitation and abuse. In this doctrinal framework, the rule of law and police and civilian aspects should be reinforced. Finally, it is important to consider what core civilian capabilities are needed in high-intensity situations and what capacities could make the most impact. Political officers and human rights officers may be obvious candidates here, but also gender and conduct/discipline officers can help the mission to achieve its objectives as well as prevent unwanted consequences. A core characteristic emerging is that the few civilian staff deployed to the field in African missions will necessarily cover several functions – for example the Stabilization Course for AU staff covers security and governance, conflict management, quick impact projects and institution-building.

As the AU experience to date indicates, the only countries that are willing to contribute troops to missions where high-intensity combat operations are likely are those with regimes in place that have a strategic interest in securing stability in that particular country or region. While this may at times be a necessity, it can also have negative implications for how the mission is perceived by some factions in the host population. The AU should thus anticipate, monitor for and be ready to proactively manage the strategic consent, legitimacy and credibility of the mission as regards the host population. Given the significance of political and civilian leadership and objectives to the African model of peace operations, especially against the backdrop of current perceptions of the security trends on the continent, Yvonne Akpasom's chapter (Chapter 8) takes stock of existing policy developments in this regard and also offers strategic recommendations for how to improve them. Urgent consideration is needed of implications of stabilization and proactive interventionism for the principles underpinning the APSA in the longer term.

Summary

The significance of the changes in African peace operations are little known outside of expert policy-making circles. Given the needed continued lead roles of African regional actors in African peace and security, it is high time to disseminate knowledge around this area much more widely than has previously been the case. This volume thus takes a comprehensive look at African peace operations and the rapidly changing context they are operating in, and considers how to improve them to respond to these challenges with greater coherence between regional and subregional actors. In the book, we engage with the following questions: What adjustments are needed for the ASF to remain relevant to changing conflict trends and to enhance the effectiveness of AU peace operations? How can the ASF's RDC concept be harmonized with the ACIRC concept? What mission scenarios are most likely to require

ASF deployments over the next decade? And on that basis, what specialized and niche capacities will the AU and regions need to develop or enhance?

Strategic recommendations are provided in the concluding chapter for how African countries may best shoulder the 'Africa rising' narrative by continuing to develop effective and legitimate security mechanisms. With the ASF due to achieve full operational capability in 2015, the AU could benefit from a strategic review of African peace operations. That could enable it to prepare for the next decade on the basis of a shared strategic vision for ASF operations that is relevant to the current and near-future context and adjusted to the strategic objectives of the AU's *Agenda 2063* and *Silencing the Guns* by 2020.

Notes

1 The ASF is partially operationalized; in March 2015 the Eastern African Standby Force was declared ready.

2 The EU is the biggest net contributor to the APSA via the African Peace Facility. Apart from traditional donors, African regional actors are increasingly negotiating partnerships and assistance packages with non-traditional donors (China, Russia, Brazil, India, etc.) (African Union 2014a).

3 In recognition of the challenges posed to the APSA, the AU PSC held its first-ever meeting at the level of heads of states and government, devoted to prevention and combating of terrorism and violent extremism (African Union 2014a).

4 With the term model, therefore, we speak of an ideal type rather than a fixed or essentialist concept.

References

African Union (2014a) *AU Peace and Security Council Meeting at Level of Heads of States and Government, 455th Meeting Communiqué, 2 Sept 2014 Nairobi*, Nairobi: African Union, au.int/en/content/peace-and-security-council-455th-meeting-level-heads-state-and-government-nairobi-kenya, accessed 13 May 2015.

— (2014b) *Progress Report of the High Level Panel on Alternative Sources of Financing the African Union, 15 July 2014, SC7749*, Addis Ababa: African Union, http://ccpau.org/wp-content/uploads/2014/03/Obasanjo-Panel-Progress-Report-Assembly-AU-18-XIX-2012-_E.pdf, accessed 18 November 2015.

— (2015a) *10th Meeting of the African Union–United Nations Joint Task Force on Peace and Security, Addis Ababa, 1 February 2015 Joint Communiqué Rev. 1*, Addis Ababa: African Union, www.peaceau.org/uploads/au-un-joint-com-01-02-2015-1.pdf, accessed 13 May 2015.

— (2015b) *Peace and Security Council 502nd Meeting, Common African Position on the UN Review of Peace Operations, Addis Ababa, 29th April 2015, PSC/PR/2(DII)*.

— (2015c) *Press Statement AU Peace and Security Council 532nd Meeting, Addis Ababa, 10 August 2015, PSC/PR/BR.(DXXXII)*.

African Union Commission (2015) *African Union Handbook*, Addis Ababa, www.nzembassy.com/webfm_send/1944, accessed 18 November 2015..

Bachmann, J. (2014) 'Policing Africa: the US mlitary and visions of crafting "good order"', *Security Dialogue*, XLV(2): 119–36.

Badmus, I. A. (2015) *The African Union's Role in Peacekeeping: Building on Lessons Learned from Security Operations*, Basingstoke: Palgrave Macmillan.

Berdal, M. and D. H. Ucko (2015) 'The use of force in UN peacekeeping operations', *RUSI Journal*, CLX(1): 6–12.

Boutellis, A. and P. D. Williams (2013) *Peace Operations, the African Union, and the United Nations: Toward More Effective Partnerships*, New York: International Peace Institute, reliefweb. int/sites/reliefweb.int/files/resources/ Peace%20Operations,%20the%20 African%20Union,%20and%20the%20 United%20Nations%20Toward%20 More%20Effective%20Partnerships.pdf, accessed 18 November 2015.

Brosig, M. (2013) 'Introduction: the African security regime complex – exploring converging actors and policies', *African Security*, VI(3/4): 171–90.

De Coning, C. (1997) 'The role of the OAU in conflict management in Africa, conflict management, peacekeeping and peace-building', in M. Malan (ed.), *Lessons for Africa from a Seminar Past*, ISS Monograph Series no. 10, Pretoria: Institute for Security Studies.

— (2014) 'Enhancing the efficiency of the ASF: the case for a shift to a just-in-time rapid response model', *Conflict Trends*, 2: 34–40.

— (2015) 'Implications of offensive and stabilisation mandates for the future of UN peacekeeping', Blog, 15 February, http://cedricdeconing.net/2015/02/15/ implications-of-offensive-and-stabilisation-mandates-for-the-future-of-un-peacekeeping, accessed 27 November 2015.

Engel, U. and J. G. Porto (eds) (2013) *Towards an African Peace and Security Regime: Continental Embeddedness, Transnational Linkages, Strategic Relevance*, Burlington: Ashgate.

— (2014) 'Imagining, implementing, and integrating the African peace and security architecture: the African Union's challenges', *African Security*, VII(3): 135–46.

Gelot, L. (2012) *Legitimacy, Peace Operations and Regional-Global Security: The African Union–United Nations Partnership in Darfur*, New York: Routledge.

Karlsrud, J. (2015) 'The UN at war: examining the consequences of peace enforcement mandates for the UN peacekeeping operations in the CAR, the DRC and Mali', *Third World Quarterly*, XXXVI(1): 40–54.

Lotze, W. (2013) *Strengthening African Peace Support Operations: Nine Lessons for the Future of the African Standby Force. ZIF Policy Briefing*, Berlin: ZIF – Centre for International Peace Operations, http://www.zif-berlin.org/ en/about-zif/news/detail/article/neues-zif-policy-briefing-strengthening-african-peace-support-operations.html, accessed 18 November 2015.

Perlo-Freeman, S. and C. Solmirano (2014) *SIPRI Fact Sheet 2014: Trends in World Military Expenditure, 2013*, Stockholm: Stockholm International Peace Research Institute.

Tardy, T. (2014) 'The reluctant peacekeeper: France and the use of force in peace operations', *Journal of Strategic Studies*, XXXVII(5): 770–92.

Tardy, T. and M. Wyss (2014) *Peacekeeping in Africa: The Evolving Security Architecture*, New York: Routledge.

UN (United Nations) (2015) *Report of the High-level Independent Panel on United Nations Peace Operations: Uniting our Strengths for Peace – Politics, Partnership and People*, 16 June, New York: United Nations, http://www. un.org/sg/pdf/HIPPO_Report_1_ June_2015.pdf, accessed 18 November 2015.

UNSC (United Nations Security Council) (2006) *Resolution 1674*, New York: United Nations.

— (2013) *Resolution 2098*, New York: United Nations Security Council.

— (2014) *Resolution 2195*, New York: United Nations.

— (2015) 'UNSC 7439th Meeting Cooperation between the United Nations and regional and subregional organizations in maintaining international peace and security', S/PV.7439, 11 May, New York.

Wallensteen, P. and A. Bjurner (2015) *Regional Organizations and Peacemakers: Challengers to the UN?*, Abingdon: Routledge.

Weiss, T. G. and M. Welz (2014) 'The UN and AU in Mali and beyond, a shotgun wedding?', *International Affairs*, 90(4): 889–905.

World Affairs Journal (2015) 'Buhari commits $100m to Lake Chad Basin fight against Boko Haram', 15 June, http://www.worldaffairsjournal.org/content/nigerias-buhari-commits-100-millionlake-chad-basin-fight-against-bokoharam, accessed 18 November 2015.

2 | Confronting hybrid threats in Africa: improving multidimensional responses

Kwesi Aning and Mustapha Abdallah

Introduction

Africa's security landscape is rapidly changing, with 'old' security threats and problems mutating and transforming into 'new' and difficult challenges. These combined threats are undermining societies and exposing the weaknesses of previously established national and regional institutions and risk and vulnerability assessment methodologies in predicting and responding to these 'new' asymmetric and hybrid security challenges. Several critical issues arise with the growing incidence of attacks by terrorist groups and the disturbing expansion of organized criminal activities. As a result, questions that need to be answered include: How are the African Union (AU) and its respective RECs' response strategies nuanced to tackle these asymmetric and hybrid security challenges? What restructuring, if any, should occur to make security institutions more responsive to the rapidly changing security environment?

This chapter examines what it perceives as evolving hybrid and asymmetric threats and their complex interconnectedness, which are increasingly posing dangerous threats to states and citizens and causing dire human and national security challenges in Africa. Focusing on threats such as terrorism and terrorist networks, transnational organized crime, the growth of illicit economies, food insecurity and health pandemics such as the Ebola virus disease (EVD), the chapter argues that, while most of these security challenges have existed and have been known in the past, what compounds their present manifestation is that they continue to mutate and transform as a result of not only the socio-economic, environmental and political dynamics within states, but also the imperatives of external politics, globally. The mutation and transformation of these threats have been dramatic, especially after the dawn of the new millennium and subsequent terrorist attacks on the United States in 2001 (Aning 2010b; Bond 2014). These developments have contributed to rendering existing countermeasures to hybrid threats at best somewhat ineffective and at worst inconsequential.

Undoubtedly, terrorism and other hybrid threats have posed real and potential dangers to human and state security, particularly within vulnerable and weak states that serve as both the incubators and the vectors for these threats. Furthermore, their continued ability to transmute and the wider ramifications and implications of such changes are placing further strains on the security apparatuses of regional and subregional organizations such as the AU's peace and security architecture and the Economic Community of West African States (ECOWAS). As a result of the potential region-wide consequences of these hybrid and asymmetric threats, and given their complex interconnectedness, it is imperative to contextualize the discussion broadly within the interrelated spheres of politics, security, economy and society. Such a broad contextualization of the nature and characteristics of these challenges will provide a more nuanced and differentiated understanding and appreciation of what national strategies and coordinated region-wide policy responses ought to be designed to address these threats. In this regard, emphasis will be placed on the need to either modify or improve the existing multidimensional approaches of the AU as well as its RECs in responding to the hybrid and asymmetric threats.

Consequently, the analyses will proceed in four sections. In section one, we discuss what we perceive as constituting these broad asymmetric and hybrid threats. One important dimension, adding to the perceived urgency of responding, is that these challenges are receiving ever more attention in national and international security discourses because they continue to manifest and transform in multiple forms and thus have become potential global threats without concerted responses. Because these threats also defy and resist conventional, unilateral approaches, countermeasures and classical tactics of warfare, they thus pose potential and real dangers to human security, states as well as regional security frameworks. Section two examines the interlinkages between hybrid and asymmetric threats and how they mutually reinforce each other. In other words, the chapter explores how the emergence or transmutation of one threat exacerbates another and/or creates the conditions for other threats to worsen. Though in the last decade Africa's multilateral institutions have designed complex response mechanisms to deal with its peace and security challenges, we argue that these threats pose particular types of response difficulties that undermine the efficacy and effectiveness of the established frameworks (African Union 2005). Consequently, the third section examines the possible implications of these threats and how they constitute a challenge to peace and security in Africa. Finally, we discuss how national and coordinated region-wide multidimensional approaches can be modified and improved, both by states and multilateral institutions such as the AU and the RECs, to address what has been characterized as 'the African security predicament' (Aning and Salihu 2013: ch. 2).

Understanding the evolving complexities of hybrid and asymmetric threats

This section discusses four interrelated threats: terrorism; transnational organized crime, and the illicit economies that it engenders; climate change and its correlation to food security; and health pandemics. The discussion on health pandemics will focus on the EVD currently considered a complex health/security emergency in West Africa, not only in the subregion but increasingly as a growing threat to regional and global security (Nigerian Federal Ministry of Health 2014; Nakamura 2014; Klein 2014).

Terrorism Terrorism is undoubtedly one of the hybrid threats confronting Africa in the twenty-first century. This assertion is confirmed by a 2012 study which concluded that, with the decentralization of threats from al-Qaeda, Africa is emerging as a new epicentre of terrorism and extremism (Gunaratna et al. 2012; Aning and Ewi 2006). Although terrorism is an 'old' security threat, references are frequently made to 'new' terrorism, especially after the Cold War when state sponsorship of terrorism began to decline (Aning 2011; Makarenko 2004: 1). The 1998 coordinated bombings of the US embassies in Nairobi, Kenya and Dar es Salaam in Tanzania were the major terrorist attacks in recent history in Africa. The almost simultaneous detonation of explosives in the two cities not only resulted in hundreds of fatalities and injuries to Kenyan, Tanzanian and American citizens, but became the harbinger of a new mode of terrorist atrocities that the world had hitherto hardly experienced on such a scale and thus attracted global condemnation (Atta-Asmoah 2009). Those two incidents brought to the fore the awareness that terrorism, which had arguably been experienced on a more limited scale in Africa, was resurfacing in a different and previously unknown form and that the West, particularly the USA, was being targeted by terrorist groups, notably al-Qaeda. The subsequent 9/11 attacks in the USA confirmed this and laid bare the fundamental shift in the nature and modus operandi of terrorists, particularly non-state actors. In other words, terrorism was branded as 'modern' or 'new' with diverse manifestations, including suicide bombing, car bombing, kidnapping of humanitarian, aid and foreign workers and schoolchildren and attacks on mosques, churches, transport terminals and hotels, among others (Vasilogambros 2013). Increasingly, the new manifestations have become more lethal, less state-centric, more networked, more organized, more willing to conduct crime for economic gains and more inclined to be motivated by religious imperatives (Aning and Amedzrator 2014; Vorrath 2014).

While five countries – Somalia, Nigeria, Mali, the southern part of Algeria and Ethiopia – have been identified as the five top countries where the threat of terrorism is rife (Gunaratna et al. 2012), the US State Department *Report on Terrorism* in 2013 indicated that, with the possible exception of southern

African countries, there is an alarming proliferation of terrorist groups in all regions in Africa, undermining societies and exposing the weaknesses of states and (sub)regional actors.

In East Africa, al-Shabaab, a notable terrorist group, has increased in strength and has persistently engaged in terrorist acts, seeking to implement sharia law in Somalia by exploiting the increasing divisions among ethnic groups and warlords (ibid.). Although Somali security forces and the AU Mission in Somalia (AMISOM) continue to pursue al-Shabaab, their failure to undertake consistent offensive operations against the group allows it to develop and carry out asymmetric attacks, including outside of Somalia (United States Department of State 2013). In 2013, for instance, al-Shabaab launched an attack against the Westgate Mall in Nairobi, Kenya, that left at least sixty-five people dead. Since October 2014, it has carried out a series of attacks in both Kenya (leading to the resignation of both the interior minister and the Inspector General of Police) and Somalia. What was disturbing about these attacks was the deliberate and callous separation of Muslims from Christians before executions took place (Spencer 2014).

Notable terrorist groups such as Boko Haram, AQIM, Ansar Dine and the Movement for Oneness and Jihad in West Africa (MUJAO) have sprung up in West Africa, utilizing the structural weaknesses in the region ostensibly to establish parallel authorities in states such as Mali and Nigeria (Aning 2012; Kieh and Kalu 2013; Tramond and Seigneur 2013; Aning and Amedzrator 2014). More disturbingly, Boko Haram is changing its tactics from hit-and-run to capturing cities, and renaming them with a view to establishing an Islamic state in north-eastern Nigeria. Mubi, a recently captured town, was renamed Madinatul Islam (City of Islam) in October 2014 (Obi n.d.). As a consequence, Rejab Gunaratna describes Boko Haram as 'a different sort of animal', seeking to fight against marginalization and establish sharia law in the northern part of Nigeria (Gunaratna et al. 2012).

In the CAR, for example, despite the deployment of 2,000 French soldiers and a 6,000-strong African Union peacekeeping mission, the 'anti-balaka' militia continues to attack AU peacekeepers, known as the African-led International Support Mission to the CAR (MISCA), hence their description as a terrorist group by the AU. And moreover, in spite of the limited threat of violent Islamist extremism and terrorism in the Democratic Republic of the Congo (DRC), the killing of twenty-one civilians in Beni Territory, North Kivu, by hacking and beheading them with machetes raised concern about the possible emergence of terrorist threats, especially given the fact that the country is vast and lacks complete state control over many of its nine contiguous boundaries (United States Department of State 2013).

The 2011 Arab Spring not only strengthened the coercive capacity of existing radical or 'jihadists' groups such as AQIM in North Africa, but also created the conditions for other groups to emerge, notably Ansar al-Sharia, with splinter groups in Benghazi and Darnah.[1] Although most of the North African countries, including Algeria, Tunisia and Egypt, face the threat of terrorism in varying dimensions, the ouster of Muammar al-Qaddafi in 2011, and the ensuing lack of state control in Libya, has particularly pigeonholed the country as a haven and strategic hub for al-Qaeda and affiliated extremist and terrorist groups. The seizure of an alleged al-Qaeda operative, Abu Anas al-Libi, by US Special Forces on 5 October 2013 was a disturbing development and indicates the ease with which al-Qaeda operatives roam freely in Libya. Ansar al-Sharia has transmuted from Katibat Ansar al-Sharia in Benghazi to Ansar al-Sharia in Libya, causing mayhem to humans and undermining state security (Okyere 2013).

Understanding the reality and challenge of organized criminality in Africa Transnational organized criminal activities (TOCs) remain one of the daunting security challenges facing Africa today. As argued by Shaw et al. (2014), although there is growing acceptance of a standardized set of definitions regarding what constitutes organized crime globally, there remains much less consensus, both by external and internal analysts, as to how the concept should be defined in the context of Africa. The seeming lack of consensus on the definition of TOCs adds to the complexity of its study given the multiple range of actors involved. Thus, within the sphere of peace and security in Africa, the United Nations Security Council (UNSC) sees organized crime as not limited to issues of drug trafficking, human trafficking, money laundering and piracy, but embracing everything from small arms proliferation to illicit mineral extraction and wildlife poaching, oil and counterfeit goods, advanced fee and internet fraud, illegal manufacture of firearms, armed robbery, and theft (ibid.; Aning 2007, 2009; UNODC 2009). The growing threat of these crimes is nothing but a reflection of observable symptoms of regional vulnerabilities characterized by bad governance, weakness of law enforcement agencies and state institutions, unemployment, poverty and porous borders (UNODC 2005).

Although all regions in Africa are confronted with the threat of TOCs in different proportions, the poorer regions, namely West Africa, Central Africa and East Africa, are mostly affected. For instance, a *Comprehensive Assessment of Drug Trafficking and Organised Crime in West and Central Africa* by the African Union in 2014 indicates that these regions in particular are in an important period of transformation in which political, economic and social shifts are being accompanied by a corresponding increase in organized crime and illicit trafficking, which are in themselves shaping both ongoing trends and the emerging nature of governance in the regions (ibid.).

With regard to drug trafficking in West Africa, two distinct trans-shipment hubs have emerged: the Guineas (Guinea and Guinea-Bissau) as one point and the Bight of Benin, which spans from Ghana to Nigeria, as the other.

Traffickers mainly from South/Latin America transport the cocaine to poorly guarded ports and airfields for onward distribution. The latest seizure in the second hub involved a Ghanaian/Austrian trafficker, Nayele Ametefe, also known as Ruby Adu-Gyamfi, arrested at Heathrow Airport in London for trafficking 12.5 kilograms of cocaine with a street value of US$5,000,000 from Kotoka Airport in Accra in late November 2014 (City People 2014).

In East Africa, the growing trend in TOCs is a reflection of both illicit markets that span continents and an underlying weakness in the rule of law. Against a background of conflict and poverty, the region produces a large and vulnerable stream of smuggled migrants, who are abused and exploited at multiple stages of their journey. In 2012, more than 100,000 people paid smugglers to transport them across the Gulf of Aden or the Red Sea to Yemen, generating an income for the boatmen of over US$15 million (UNODC 2013). Heroin seizures have increased lately, while annual poaching activities produce between 56 and 154 metric tons of illicit ivory, of which two-thirds (37 tons) is destined for Asia, worth around US$30 million in 2011 (ibid.; Gastrow 2011). In Somalia, pirates brought in an estimated US$150 million in 2011, which is equivalent to almost 15 per cent of its GDP (UNODC 2013).

Climate change and food security Climate change has been identified as one of the leading human and environmental (McMichael 2004) crises of the twenty-first century globally (Tadesse 2010). But Africa is particularly affected owing to its geographical position and considerably limited adaptive capacity. As African states continue to depend largely on the weather and the soil for their sustenance, it makes them extremely vulnerable to ecological stresses and strains, exacerbated by widespread poverty and the existing low levels of development (UNEP n.d.). As a result, the impacts of climate change on food and water security have become glaring, constituting a potential source of insecurity in the region, and have been cited as a major contributory factor in the dwindling harvests in the subregion (ibid.). It is further estimated that, by 2020, between 75 and 250 million people in Africa will be exposed to increased water stress owing to climate change (ibid.). In some countries, yields from rain-fed agriculture could be reduced by up to 50 per cent (ibid.). Agricultural production, including access to food, in many African countries is projected to be severely compromised (ibid.).

Currently, the price of basic staples such as rice and cassava has doubled in Sierra Leone and Liberia (Sy and Copley 2014). But the Sahelian countries such as Mauritania, Mali, Niger and Burkina Faso appear to be the hardest hit. Refugee inflows following the Libyan crisis and the Tuareg rebellion in Mali have intensified the food security situation, aggravating socio-economic conditions in the Sahel. The influx of over 400,000 returnees from Libya to Niger, Mali, Chad and Mauritania has further exacerbated the situation. Consequently, over one million people are currently at risk from the food crisis in the Sahel region of West Africa, including 1 million children, who are at risk of severe malnutrition (Aning et al. 2012). This has created a humanitarian crisis and negatively impacted on the capacity of governments, humanitarian agencies and non-governmental organizations working in the areas. Appropriate adaptation and mitigation strategies remain weak in virtually all these countries. This means any major environmental disaster will most likely have catastrophic consequences for affected states and their societies.

Health pandemics in Africa Threats to the public health security of states involve the emergence and spread of infectious diseases, and the steady and increasing rise in non-infectious diseases (Itam and Adindu 2012). To this end, protection from health threats is widely recognized as an important non-traditional security issue, often caused by infectious agents. Whether they affect humans, animals or crops, infectious diseases continue to be a fundamental impediment to both economic development and human health in Africa (Rweyemamu et al. 2006). They emerge naturally at the human–animal interface, but may also be caused by chemicals, toxins, radiation or deliberate acts of terrorism (ibid.).

Historically, Africa has faced and continues to be challenged by many infectious diseases, including the current EVD pandemic (Formenty et al. 2003). Out of the ten deadliest diseases in Africa – syphilis, meningitis, whooping cough, measles, tuberculosis, HIV/AIDS, tetanus, diarrhoea, malaria and pneumonia and other lower respiratory tract infections – the first six are infectious.

Although some of the identified infectious diseases have been contained through the development of vaccines, HIV/AIDS and Ebola remain major public health issues because of continued mutation of the viruses and lack of scientific breakthrough in terms of vaccines. Experts in health and economics increasingly agree that it is infectious diseases that play the greatest role in Africa's underdevelopment rather than issues such as the slave trade, colonialism and conflicts (Sidlibe 2009). Although this view may be contested owing to the changing dynamics of threats, the argument cannot be completely discounted. The situation is largely a result of inadequate logistics and health infrastructure, prevalent in many African states. Infectious diseases have thus often assumed pandemic proportions when they occur, raising human and national security concerns. HIV/AIDS, for instance, has posed severe humanitarian concerns to Africa, especially over the last two or more decades. Three out of four deaths in Africa are caused by infectious disease, and with its 11 per cent of the world population, Africa has 60 per cent of people living with HIV (ibid.).

Following from this, Sidlibe noted in 2009 that 'if Africa remains poorly equipped to respond to [the] AIDS pandemic of today, how can Africa be ready for the health challenges of tomorrow?' (ibid.). Predictably, four years down the line in 2013, Africa began to grapple with and continues to face the Ebola pandemic. As reflected in Sidibe's 2009 speech, not only is the continent poorly equipped to contain the threat, but the world at large is overwhelmed and struggling to find a vaccine to curb the spread of the epidemic.

Reiterating this fear of future epidemics, the World Bank president, Jim Yong Kim, noted that 'even as we focus intensely on the Ebola emergency response, we must also invest in public health infrastructure, institutions and systems to prepare for the next epidemic, which could spread much more quickly, kill even more people and potentially devastate the global economy' (UN 2014).

The above statement summarizes the gravity of the EVD threat today, and at the same time underscores the need to prepare for future threats as Guinea, Liberia, Mali and Sierra Leone are currently facing the threat, with over 5,000 people killed and more than 10,000 infected. Other countries, including Nigeria, Senegal, Mali, the USA, Spain and Germany, have also reported cases, indicating the possibility of its spread to other parts of the globe. Consequently, during the 2014 UN General Assembly meeting, Barack Obama, the US president, highlighted the need for UN member states to make individual and collective efforts in fighting the EVD. In pursuance of this, he indicated that: 'stopping Ebola is a priority for the United States [...] We'll do our part. We will continue to lead, but this has to be a priority for everybody. [owing to its global ramifications]'

Undoubtedly, the rapid spread of the disease in Liberia and Sierra Leone can be attributed to the post-conflict challenges of weak infrastructure, reflected in the lack of capacity of these states to contain and address the current Ebola threat, and by extension lack of financial resources and institutional capacity in the wider African continent. In view of the threat Ebola poses to the West African subregion, and its wider ramifications on the continent and the world at large, efforts are being made at various level to curb the threat.[2]

The evolving nexus among hybrid threats

Hybrid threats continue to evolve. In the early 1990s, terrorism and organized crime were perceived to be driven by different motivations: terrorists were perceived to have political, ideological, religious or ethnic goals and organized criminals mostly economic goals. Terrorism was thus seen as perpetuating political violence rather than engaging in criminality (Liang 2011). However, the post-Cold War international political dynamic has brought to the fore convergence of their operations, especially as state sponsorship for terrorism began to dwindle in the 1990s, making this the decade in which the crime–terror nexus was consolidated (Makarenko 2004; Shelley et al. 2005). For instance, the former Liberian president Charles Taylor allegedly harboured al-Qaeda members who had come to trade in diamonds from Sierra Leone (Lansana 2013; Aning et al. 2013; Etannibi 2013).[3] Two known al-Qaeda members bought diamonds and tried to buy surface-to-air missiles in Liberia (Dietrich et al. 2013). Several al-Qaeda affiliates engaged in similar activities, including al-Qaeda in the Islamic Maghreb (AQIM) and al-Shabaab in Somalia. In particular, al-Shabaab moved from taxing Somali pirates' ransom revenues to dispatching its own fighters to attack ships in its own skiffs, particularly targeting American ships (UNODC 2013).

Increasingly today, significant numbers of terrorist groups in Africa are engaged in some form of organized crime or illicit economic activities. Similarly, a growing number of organized crime cartels are engaging in political violence. TOCs have thus become a major revenue source for terrorist groups worldwide. Undoubtedly, trafficking drugs remains the most common criminal act that is uniting organized criminals with terrorists. Consequently, these groups are being labelled by law enforcement agencies with new terms such as narco-terrorists, narco-guerrillas and narco-fundamentalists.[4]

Apart from the post-Cold War political dynamics, a number of other factors should be mentioned. Globalization, the communication revolution through the internet, the end of the Cold War and the 'global war on terror' have contributed to the growing nexus and cooperation between the two threats. In Africa, for instance, globalization is creating conditions where terror–crime cooperation is exploiting the weakness of borders. AQIM, for instance, has collaborated with local Tuareg and Berabiche ethnic groups to traffic cocaine, hashish and counterfeit tobacco. Militant groups have also established networks with South American narcotics traffickers, which has substantially improved their potential to raise income for extremist activities; enabled them to learn more professional methods of contraband transport; and provided access to light- and medium-weight arms that can easily be packaged along with the cocaine (Aning and Amedzrator 2014).

The nexus of threats is also reflected in climate change, food security and health pandemics. Indeed, most diseases in Africa are environmentally related. In other words, poor management of the environment has created conditions for most diseases to emerge and spread within and across borders. The climate challenge characterized by increasing desertification and erratic rainfall, especially in the Sahel region of Africa, has created food shortages in many states, namely Mali, Niger, Burkina Faso and Mauritania. As indicated already, prices of basic staples such as rice have risen in the Sahel, as an unintended consequence of the Arab Spring, creating refugees and aggravating socio-economic conditions in the region (Sy and Copley 2014).

The food crisis has worsened owing to the outbreak of Ebola, reducing the number of people and man-hours on the farms. Already, staple crops such as rice and maize are reportedly being scaled back owing to shortages in farm labour, with potential 'catastrophic' effects on food security (Aning and Amedzrator 2014). The growing crisis has come about as a result of the huge dependence on agriculture as an economic activity in the region (ibid.). As a consequence, suspected or infected Ebola patients who are under quarantine are threatening to terminate their quarantine because of lack of food supplies. This is a worrying development, as it presages the further spread of the virus.

Security/economic implications of the hybrid threat nexus in Africa

While the identified hybrid threats constitute security challenges in their own right, the growing nexus between one and the other is creating conditions and dynamics that perpetuate war, conflicts and insurgency across the continent. Following the Arab Spring that led to the ousting of Muammar al-Qaddafi, criminal networks and returnee migrants to the Sahel joined forces with insurgent groups such as the National Movement for the Liberation of the Azawad (MNLA) and other disaffected groups mobilized in Mali to stage an uprising against the state, utilizing traditional ties with local communities. Mutual partnerships were also forged with criminal networks to consolidate gains from an emerging criminal economy through kidnapping, hostage-taking, smuggling of contraband goods and tax collection from smugglers (Aning and Amedzrator 2014). Although elections have been held following the ousting of Amadou Toumani Touré in 2012, weaknesses in state institutions have exacerbated conditions in which criminal networks continue to collaborate with militant groups to perpetrate crime and undermine state security (Aning et al. 2014). In this regard, it has increasingly become the trend for militant and extremist groups to provide safe passage and protection to traffickers in exchange for an agreed percentage of the total face value of the trafficked goods (Aning 2010a).

In Libya, the rapid emergence of terrorist groups such Katibat Ansar al-Sharia in Benghazi and its subsequent transmutation into Ansar al-Sharia in Libya has created conditions in which organized criminal behaviour is having a decisive impact on the state. As a consequence of this, networks and alliances and four interconnected markets –for weapons, migrants, drugs and the smuggling of subsidized goods in and out of Libya – have become conspicuously prevalent (Aning and Amedzrator 2014). As Libya strives to attain political and economic stabilization during its political transition phase, the widespread prevalence of weapons has completely changed the nature of the game in Libya. At present, the complex interconnections between terrorist groups and criminal networks are occupying spaces created by the absence of the state.

The economic impact has manifested itself with the continued spread of the EVD and the worsening food security situation, especially in the four affected countries. Before the outbreak, Sierra Leone and Liberia were making remarkable economic progress. For instance, in 2013 Sierra Leone and Liberia ranked second and sixth among the top ten countries with the highest GDP growth in the world (although their base levels of GDP were very small to begin with) (Sy and Copley 2014). While Guinea was growing rather slowly at 2.5 per cent in 2013, there was expectation for higher growth based on iron ore projects that were to be undertaken with international investors (ibid.). However, the intensification of the EVD partly affected investor confidence in the region and began to hinder contributions to future growth.

As a result, the economic impact of EVD has been felt in several sectors of the economies of the affected states, but severely in the agricultural sector. According to the Food and Agriculture Organization (FAO), agriculture accounts for 57 per cent of Sierra Leone's GDP, 39 per cent of Liberia's and 20 per cent of Guinea's (ibid.). Already, the price of the staple crops – for instance, cassava – has more than doubled in some places in Liberia (ibid.). In Sierra Leone, the agricultural sector contributes half of the country's GDP and employs 2.5 per cent of the country's workforce (IRIN 2014). As of October 2014, the economic impact of the EVD was reflected in a 30 per cent drop in GDP.

Beyond this, international investors and multinationals are scaling back and construction activities are massively affected. The service and transport sectors continue to slow down, eroding government revenues. The government has had to boost expenditure, channelling US$13.7 million to the Ebola fight amid a shrinking budget (ibid.).

Multidimensional responses to hybrid threats

Undoubtedly, addressing hybrid threats with a single approach will not only be difficult and counterproductive, but to a large extent impossible owing to their complex interlinkages. Developing innovative means and improving on the existing multidimensional approaches, based on the changing dynamics of the threat, are critical. But more important are coherence and synergy between and among states, subregional and regional organizations – for example, the AU and the RECs. In this regard, the following measures need consideration.

Revision of response mechanisms An analysis of the threats above reveals complex interlinkages and convergence of characteristics. While most of the threats may originate from one source, they often assume a transnational character, exposing the weaknesses of state and regional institutional capacity. Thus, the existing mechanisms and approaches by the AU and the RECs need to be constantly adapted and revised to reflect the dynamics of emerging threats. Currently, there is a need to involve relevant non-state actors in playing a complementary role because many sources of security threats are located in the local communities and far removed from the control of state institutions and regional security agencies. For instance, in most of the Sahel states, especially in Mali, radical groups and their complex networks are increasingly establishing bases in local communities. It is, therefore, imperative to involve other non-core state institutions in providing hybrid peace and security. In this regard, civil society organizations, traditional and religious leaders and local peace actors will play significant roles.

Coordination of efforts and existing strategies Coordination of efforts, especially in the area of intelligence-gathering and information-sharing, is absolutely imperative among states on the one hand, and between the AU and the RECs on the other hand. Despite the establishment of the AU's Continental Early Warning System (CEWS), the ECOWAS Early Warning Network (ECOWARN) and the Conflict Early Warning and Response Mechanism (CEWARN) of the Intergovernmental Agency for Development (IGAD), the link between early warning and response mechanisms remains weak. The capacity to respond is often lacking, both at the AU and the REC levels, despite clear warning signals. It is in this regard that the AU has established the ACIRC. Although it is yet to be endorsed by all member states and be operationalized, it aims at responding to conflicts and emerging threats more rapidly than the current ASF can do. For this mechanism to be effective, however, the AU should improve its coordination with the RECs in terms of early warning and the coordinated rapid response should be linked to the professional advice of the Committee of Chiefs of Defence Staff, both at regional and subregional levels.

With regard to the threat of terrorism and Boko Haram, for instance, Niger, Nigeria, Chad and Cameroon are coordinating efforts and have deployed troops as part of a multinational force to fight this threat. Together with Benin, these nations have agreed to speed up the creation of a headquarters for the force and have military battalions deployed to their respective borders. This effort is being complemented at the ECOWAS level, with Committee of Chiefs of the Defence Staff meetings held under the aegis of the president of Ghana, John Dramani Mahama, and the current president of the ECOWAS Commission.

Currently, there are multiple strategies being adopted by states and regional organizations to respond to evolving terrorism and other threats in Africa, but there is no overall comprehensive strategy that seeks to address the complex interlinkages between terrorism and criminal networks. Among others, the Joint EU–Africa Strategy, the United Nations Strategy for the Sahel, the African Union Strategy (MISAHEL) and the ECOWAS Sahel Strategy exist to counter the threat of terrorism. At the state level, countries including the USA and France have counterterrorism measures. In particular, France's counterterrorism strategy in Africa and the Sahel covers states such as Chad, Mali, Burkina Faso, Niger and Côte d'Ivoire. While these strategies are all intended to contribute to addressing the existing challenges, the question is which of the existing strategies should be considered pre-eminent? How do we coordinate and strengthen the coherence of the various initiatives under one comprehensive strategy for the Sahel to address the evolving networks of criminal and terrorist groups? In many instances, the various initiatives become counterproductive as they fail to properly identify the underlying dynamics of the threats as well as the unintended consequences of these strategies. There is no doubt that stand-alone strategies of states and organizations are underpinned by diverse interests, and until such interests are coordinated under one umbrella, the implementation of the strategies will be less effective or face practical implementation challenges. In this regard, coordinated strategies of the AU and the RECs based on their early warning information should be considered paramount.

Improved infrastructure The raging Ebola pandemic in Africa and the consequences in terms of the number of deaths indicate existing poor infrastructure in many African states as well as the inadequate capacity of organizations such as ECOWAS and the AU to respond to such complex emergencies.

As argued by the World Bank president, Jim Yong Kim, future disasters could spread much more quickly, kill even more people and potentially devastate the global economy. As such, the AU and the RECs should prioritize the improvement of infrastructure in their development agenda. But what is critical in the current circumstances is to support the West African subregion in improving its infrastructural base, especially health infrastructure given the menace of Ebola in the subregion. This is necessary for the region to strengthen its disaster management capabilities in order to forestall future disasters, whether rain, fire or many others.

Independent sources of funding The capacity of the AU and the RECs to respond to emerging threats will be dependent largely on independent sources of funding. Currently, the AU as well as the RECs depend hugely on external funds for responding to threats. In most cases, when the interests of external funders diverge from those of the AU and the RECs, the release of funds is likely to be delayed unduly and consequently hamper the effectiveness of the response mechanisms in Africa. This approach needs to change with the creation of an independent source of funds that can be readily accessed and utilized during emergencies.

Increased training and capacity-building The AU and the RECs should invest in and increase attention to the training of youth on the misconceptions relating to 'jihad', which has become a springboard for engaging in radicalization and militancy across many countries in the region. However, for such training to be effective, efforts should be made to ensure that state institutions are effective in addressing governance challenges such as corruption, unemployment and inequality, among others.

Institutional/legal and structural reforms The AU as well as the RECs should ensure that member states adhere to the principles contained in the African Charter on Democracy, Elections and Governance and refrain from manipulating constitutions for their personal interests as opposed to the interests of states. The failure of the AU and ECOWAS to punish Blaise Compaoré for manipulating the Burkinabé constitution and overtly endorsing him as a chief mediator were partly the underlying reasons for the recent protests that led to his removal.

Conclusion

This chapter has illustrated the growing complexities of hybrid and asymmetric threats and their impacts on national institutions and subregional as well as regional security architectures in Africa. While all regions in Africa are affected by the continued transformation of these threats, weaker and vulnerable states and regions are mostly affected, exposing the weaknesses of regional security mechanisms and by extension the AU as a continental body. As Africa charts a new course in its peace operations, it is imperative to interrogate and explore new ways of improving the existing response mechanisms so as to confront emerging hybrid and asymmetric threats on the continent.

Notes

1 Ansar al-Sharia (partisans of Islamic law – sharia) is a Salafist-jihadist militia based in Benghazi. Ansar al-Sharia initially manifested as a revolutionary brigade during the 2011 Libyan revolution and gained prominence following the death of Muammar al-Qaddafi. While the security situation continued to worsen in Libya, Ansar al-Sharia in Libya (ASL) took advantage of the lack of state control by building local communal ties, which strengthened its ability to operate in more locations than Benghazi. In the aftermath of the attack on the US consulate in Benghazi, a major rebranding began by changing the group's name from Katibat Ansar al-Sharia in Benghazi to Ansar al-Sharia in Libya. See TRAC (n.d.).

2 At the global level, the UN Mission for Ebola Emergency Response (UNMEER) has been established in Accra, with a preliminary funding proposal of US$49.9 million for the rest of the year, while the UN Office for the Coordination of Humanitarian Affairs (OCHA) has raised US$257 million – or 26 per cent of the $988 million that it needs to respond to the outbreak of the epidemic. On 30 October 2014, the World Bank president, Jim Yong Kim, confirmed an additional $100 million in funding to be directed towards speeding up the deployment of foreign health workers to Guinea, Liberia and Sierra Leone – making the Bank's total pledges US$500 million. According to current UN estimates, about 5,000 international medical, training and support personnel are needed in the three countries over the coming months, including 700–1,000 foreign health workers, to treat patients in the Ebola treatment centres. At the subregional level, the Authority of Heads of State and Government has directed the ECOWAS Commission, in liaison with the West African Health Organization (WAHO), to adopt a regional approach to containing and managing the Ebola outbreak. To this end, the establishment of a solidarity fund has been agreed.

Some countries and institutions in and outside the region have begun to commit themselves to eradicating the virus. For example, Nigeria has contributed US$3,500,000 as follows: US$1,000,000 to Guinea, US$500,000 to Liberia, US$500,000 to Sierra Leone, US$500,000 to the West African Health Organization (WAHO) and US$1,000,000 to the ECOWAS Pool Fund for Ebola. More financial support from other ECOWAS members and development partners is needed in this regard.

3 It must be emphasized that in several West African states, this nexus has been proved.

4 Narco-terrorism, for example, could be defined as the use of drug trafficking to finance and advance the political and ideological objectives of non-state actors, criminal groups and terrorists in such a way that they threaten the rule of law, the state and the region.

References

African Union (2005) *Common African Defence and Security Policy*, pages.au.int/sites/default/files/Solemn_Declaration_on_CADSP_0.pdf, accessed 9 December 2014.

Aning, K. (2007) *Africa: Confronting Complex Threats*, New York: International Peace Academy, africacenter.org/wp-content/uploads/2007/07/Africa-Confronting-Complex-Threats.pdf, accessed 18 November 2015.

— (2009) *Organized Crime in West Africa: Options for EU Engagement*, Stockholm: International IDEA, www.idea.int/resources/analysis/loader.cfm?csmodule=security/getfile&pageid=37849, accessed 18 November 2015.

— (2010a) *Potential New Hotspots for Extremism and Opportunities to Mitigate the Danger. The case of the Sahel*, Pluscarden Programme Conference, Oxford: St Antony's College, works.bepress.com/kwesi_aning/8, accessed 18 November 2015.

— (2010b) 'Security, war on terror and ODA', *Critical Studies on Terrorism*, III(2): 7–26.

— (2011) 'Security links between trafficking and terrorism in the Sahel', in *Africa South of the Sahara*, London: Routledge.

— (2012) 'Confronting the Boko Haram challenge to Nigeria: exploring options for a peaceful settlement', *Stability Operations*, VIII(1).

Aning, K. and L. Amedzrator (2014) 'The economics of militancy and Islamist extremism in the Sahel', in CSIS (Canadian Security Intelligence Service), *Political Stability and Security in West and North Africa*, Toronto: CSIS.

Aning, K. and M. Ewi (2006) 'Assessing the role of the African Union in preventing and combating terrorism in Africa', *African Security Review*, XV(3): 32–46.

Aning, K. and N. Salihu (2013) 'The African security predicament', in J. J. Hentz (ed.), *Routledge Handbook of African Security*, London: Routledge.

Aning, K., F. Aubyn and F. Edu-Afful (2014) *Mali – a Horizon Study*, Cranfield: Cranfield University.

Aning, K., F. Okyere and M. Abdallah (2012) *Addressing Emerging Security Threats in Post-Gaddafi Sahel and the ECOWAS Response to the Malian Crisis*, Accra: Kofi Annan International Peacekeeping Training Centre, www.kaiptc.org/Publications/Policy-Briefs/Policy-Briefs/Addressing-Emerging-Security-Threats-in-Post-Gadda.aspx, accessed 18 November 2015.

Aning, K., J. Pokoo and S. Kwarkye (2013) 'Ghana', in C. Kavanagh (ed.), *Getting Smart and Scaling Up: Responding to the Impact of Organized Crime on Governance in Developing Countries*, New York: New York University.

Atta-Asmoah, A. (2009) 'Transnational and domestic terrorism in Africa: any linkages?', in W. Okumu and A. Botha (eds), *Domestic Terrorism in Africa: Defining, Addressing and Understanding its Impact on Human Security*, Pretoria: Institute for Security Studies.

Bond (2014) *Conflict Security, and Official Development Assistance (ODA): Issues for NGO Advocacy*, www.bond.org.uk/data/files/resources/331/gsdpaper.pdf, accessed 3 December 2014.

City People (2014) 'Cocaine saga: how Ghanaian socialite Nayele Ametefeh was arrested with 12.5kg of cocaine', *City People*, 26 November, citypeoplegroup.org/i/cocaine-saga-how-ghanaian-socialite-nayele-ametefehs-was-arrested-with-12-5kg-of-cocaine/, accessed 2 December 2014.

Dietrich, C., C. Fithen and L. Gberie (2013) *Final report of the Panel of Experts on Liberia submitted pursuant to paragraph 5 (f) of Security Council resolution 2079 (2012)*, New York: United Nations Security Council, www.securitycouncilreport.org/atf/cf/%7B65BFCF9B-6D27-4E9C-8CD3-CF6E4FF96FF9%7D/s_2013_683.pdf, accessed 18 November 2015.

Etannibi, E. O. A. (ed.) (2013) *The Impact of Organised Crime on Governance in West Africa*, Abuja: Friedrich Ebert Stiftung.

Formenty, P. et al. (2003) 'Outbreak of Ebola haemorrhagic fever in the Republic of the Congo, 2003: a new strategy?', Médecine Tropicale: revue du Corps de santé colonial, LXIII(3): 291–5.

Gastrow, P. (2011) *Termites at Work*, New York: International Peace Institute, theglobalobservatory.org/wp-content/uploads/2011/10/pdfs_toc_kenya_comp_proof.pdf, accessed 18 November 2015.

Gunaratna, R. et al. (2012) *Understanding the Current and Emerging Threat of Terrorism in East Africa. ICPVTR Visit to Kenya, Ethiopia and Somaliland 2012*, Singapore: International Centre for Political Violence and Terrorism Research, www.pvtr.org/pdf/Report/RSIS_ICPVTR%20Visit%20to%20E.

Africa%20Report%202012.pdf, accessed 7 December 2014.

IRIN (2014) 'Ebola's economic impact hits Sierra Leone citizens', IRIN, 18 September, www.irinnews.org/report/100629/ebola-s-economic-impact-hits-sierra-leone-citizens, accessed 18 November 2014.

Itam, H. I. and A. Adindu (2012) 'Health security in Africa and quality of health services', *College of Medical Sciences*, II(11): 43–50.

Kieh, G. K. and K. Kalu (eds) (2013) *West Africa and the US War on Terror*, New York: Routledge.

Klein, B. (2014) 'Ebola is a "national security priority," Obama says', CNN, 8 September, edition.cnn.com/2014/09/07/politics/ebola-national-security-obama/, accessed 9 December 2014.

Lansana, G. (2013) 'State officials and their involvement in drug trafficking in West Africa: preliminary findings', West Africa Commission on Drugs (WACD) Background Paper no. 5, Geneva: Kofi Annan Foundation, www.wacommissionondrugs.org/wp-content/uploads/2014/01/State-Officials-and-Drug-Trafficking-2013-12-03.pdf, accessed 18 November 2015.

Liang, S. C. (2011) 'Shadow networks: the growing nexus of terrorism and organised crime', GCSP Policy Paper no. 20, Geneva: Geneva Centre for Security Policy, http://mercury.ethz.ch/serviceengine/Files/ISN/133082/ipublicationdocument_singledocument/f15187ca-e9dd-473d-bc7b-eb99b835c3c2/en/Policy+Paper+20.pdf, accessed 18 November 2015.

Makarenko, T. (2004) 'The crime–terror continuum: tracing the interplay between transnational organised crime and terrorism', *Global Crime*, VI(1): 129–45.

McMichael, A. J. (2004) 'Environmental and social influences on emerging infectious diseases: past, present and future', *Philosophical Transitions of the Royal Society of London Series B Biological Sciences*, CCCLIX(1447): 1049–1452.

Nakamura, D. (2014) 'Obama: Ebola is "growing threat to regional and global security"', *Washington Post*, 25 September, www.washingtonpost.com/politics/obama-ebola-is-growing-threat-to-regional-and-global-security/2014/09/25/e9a65d54-44c0-11e4-b47c-f5889e061e5f_story.html, accessed 9 December 2014.

Nigerian Federal Ministry of Health (2014) *Ebola a security issue*, www.health.gov.ng/index.php/component/content/article/9-uncategorised/195-ebola-a-security-issue-ecowas-president, accessed 9 December 2014.

Obi, L. (n.d.) 'Boko Haram renames captured Adamawa Town, Mubi, "City of Islam"', *Mangrove Reporters*, www.mangrovereporters.com/index.php/general-news/local/item/5491-boko-haram-renames-captured-adamawa-town-mubi-city-of-islam/5491-boko-haram-renames-captured-adamawa-town-mubi-city-of-islam, accessed 14 November 2014.

Okyere, F. (2013) *The Legacy of UN Military Intervention and State-building in Libya*, Accra: Kofi Annan International Peacekeeping Training Centre, http://www.kaiptc.org/Publications/Policy-Briefs/Policy-Briefs/KAIPTC-Policy-Brief-2---The-Legacy-of-UN-Military-.aspx, accessed 18 November 2015.

Rweyemamu, M., W. Otim-Nape and D. Serwadda (2006) *Infectious Diseases: Preparing for the Future. Africa*, London: Office of Science and Innovation, www.gov.uk/government/uploads/system/uploads/attachment_data/file/294810/06-1768-infectious-diseases-africa.pdf, accessed 18 November 2015.

Shaw, M., T. Reitano and M. Hunter (2014) *A Comprehensive Assessment of Drug Trafficking and Organised Crime in West and Central Africa*, Addis Ababa: African Union, http://www.globalinitiative.net/download/general/subsaharan-africa/Organized%20Crime%20in%20West%20and%20Central%20Africa%20-%20July%202014%20-%20Full.pdf, accessed 18 November 2015.

Shelley, L. I. et al. (2005) 'Methods and motives: exploring links between transnational organised crime and international terrorism', *Trends in Organised Crime*, IX(2): 2–114.

Sidlibe, M. (2009) *The challenges of pandemics for the development of Africa*, Geneva: UNAIDS, www.unaids.org/sites/default/files/media_asset/20090527_ms_africandialogue_au_en_0.pdf, accessed 18 November 2015.

Spencer, R. (2014) 'Kenya: jihadists separate Muslims from Christians, murder 36 Christians', Jihad Watch, 2 December, www.jihadwatch.org/2014/12/kenya-jihadists-separate-muslims-from-christians-murder-36-christians, accessed 19 February 2015.

Sy, A. and A. Copley (2014) *Understanding the Economic Effects of the 2014 Ebola Outbreak in West Africa*, Washington, DC: Brookings Institution, www.brookings.edu/blogs/africa-in-focus/posts/2014/10/01-ebola-outbreak-west-africa-sy-copley, accessed 17 November 2014.

Tadesse, D. (2010) *The impact of climate change in Africa*, Addis Ababa: Institute for Security Studies, www.issafrica.org/uploads/Paper220.pdf, accessed 18 November 2015.

TRAC (Terrorism Research & Analysis Consortium) (n.d.) 'Ansar al-Sharif in Libya (ASL)', www.trackingterrorism.org/group/ansar-al-sharia-libya-asl?ip_login_no_cache=5c9edfe952454afe007ca907d27b3dc7, accessed 12 November 2014.

Tramond, O. and P. Seigneur (2013) 'Early lessons from France's Operation Serval in Mali', *Army Magazine*, LXIII(6): 40–43.

UN (United Nations) (2014) 'UN Ebola response in West Africa to be bolstered by increase in World Bank funding', UN News Centre, 30 October, www.un.org/apps/news/story. asp?NewsID=49207#.VVZNTzZU7TZ, accessed 10 November 2014.

UNEP (United Nations Environment Programme) (n.d.) *Fact sheet – climate change in Africa – what is at stake?*, UNEP, www.unep.org/ roa/amcen/docs/AMCEN_Events/ climate-change/2ndExtra_15Dec/ FACT_SHEET_CC_Africa.pdf, accessed 10 November 2014.

United States Department of State, Bureau of Counterterrorism (2013) *Country Report on Terrorism 2013*, www.state. gov/j/ct/, accessed April 2014.

UNODC (United Nations Office on Drugs and Crime) (2005) *Transnational Organized Crime in the West African Region*, Vienna: UNODC, https:// www.unodc.org/pdf/transnational_ crime_west-africa-05.pdf, accessed 18 November 2015.

— (2009) *Transnational Trafficking and the Rule of Law in West Africa: A Threat Assessment*, Vienna: UNODC,
https://www.unodc.org/documents/ data-and-analysis/Studies/West_ Africa_Report_2009.pdf, accessed 18 November 2015.

— (2013) *Transnational Organized Crime in Eastern Africa: A Threat Assessment*, Vienna: UNODC, https://www.unodc. org/documents/data-and-analysis/ Studies/TOC_East_Africa_2013.pdf, accessed 18 November 2015.

Vasilogambros, M. (2013) 'Soft targets remain vulnerable to terrorist attacks', *National Journal*, 19 April, www. nationaljournal.com/nationalsecurity/ soft-targets-remain-vulnerable-to-terrorist-attacks-20130419, accessed 7 December 2014.

White House (2014) 'Remarks by President Obama at U.N. Meeting on Ebola', The White House, 25 September, https://www.whitehouse. gov/the-press-office/2014/09/25/ remarks-president-obama-un-meeting-ebola, accessed 27 November 2015.

Vorrath, J. (2014) 'From war to illicit economies: organised crime and state-building in Liberia and Sierra Leone', SWP Research Paper no. 13, pp. 5–30.

3 | Stabilization missions and mandates in African peace operations: implications for the ASF?

Solomon A. Dersso

Introduction

As the African Union's (AU's) experience in deploying and conducting peace operations has expanded, the scope and nature of tasks they are mandated and called on to perform have also witnessed major changes. Unlike many of the AU's early peace operations, recent missions have been assigned responsibilities for undertaking stabilization activities and roles in the host countries. These developments have major policy implications. This is particularly the case with respect to African peace operations doctrine and to the form that the ASF takes for operational readiness. The purpose of this chapter is accordingly to examine what kind of implications the AU's missions with stabilization mandates have on the ASF concept and the adjustments, if any, that need to be made in the ongoing efforts to have the ASF operationally ready.

In this context, a very good point of departure for undertaking this exercise is to conduct a brief review of the context that has given rise to the disconnect between the ASF and the operations that the AU has deployed and run thus far, necessitating the need for reform of the ASF.

Context

One of the major changes in the peace and security landscape of Africa in the past decade has been the emergence of the AU as a major actor seeking and asserting leadership in the maintenance of peace and security on the continent. During this period, the AU has been faced with the twin challenges of institution-building and of deploying various initiatives to address the various peace and security challenges witnessed in different parts of the continent.

With respect to institution-building, the AU's major area of engagement has been the establishment and operationalization of the APSA, consisting of the norms and operational structures necessary for the maintenance of peace and security (Dersso 2010b). One of the constituent elements of the institutional dimension of the APSA is the ASF. The ASF, meant to serve as the peace operations and intervention instrument of the AU, is envisaged as being 'composed of Standby multidisciplinary contingents with civilian and military components in their countries of origin and ready for rapid deployment at appropriate notice' (African Union 2002: Article 13). The effort of translating the ASF concept into an institutional reality and achieving the operational readiness of the ASF has been under way since 2003 and is still ongoing.[1]

Simultaneously, the various conflicts and crisis situations that have emerged on the continent mean that the AU is regularly called on to respond before the various components of the APSA, including the ASF, have been ready for deployment. Indeed, parallel to the efforts of preparing the ASF for operational readiness, the AU's role in deploying peace operations in response to a number of conflict situations has increased exponentially. The major ones of such recent operations include the AU Mission to Somalia (AMISOM), the African-led International Support Mission to Mali (AFISMA) and the African-led International Support Mission to the CAR (MISCA). These operations have been deployed and conducted in response to the prevailing conditions in the areas of their deployment. Not unsurprisingly, the efforts of preparing the ASF for operational readiness and the actual peace operations of the AU have been pursued separately. As a result, one of the major questions with respect to the preparation of the ASF for operational readiness is what lessons should be drawn for the ASF from the experience of the AU's missions thus far. It is in this context that the question of the implications of stabilization mandates and missions for the ASF also arises.

Stabilization mandates and operations

Although there is no established and single understanding of stabilization, it is understood in this context to refer to the mandate and tasks of peace operations whose main objective covers the elimination or neutralization of identified 'spoiler' armed groups and the restoration or extension of state authority to territories under the control of such armed groups. This largely captures the emerging trend and understanding of stabilization. In this emerging understanding, stabilization, as articulated in a recent article by John Karlsrud, 'is about using military means to stabilize a country, often with all necessary means to neutralize potential "spoilers" to a conflict' (Karlsrud 2015: 40, 42). One of the defining elements of stabilization mandates and operations is accordingly the strategic use of force and hence the involvement of offensive combat operations.

Demands of stabilization mandates and missions[2]

Despite the increasing demand of the conflict environment for stabilization operations and the AU's initial experience in the deployment of peace operations with stabilization mandates and tasks, there is no established conceptual or doctrinal framework that articulates the essence of stabilization mandates and missions. There is also very little by way of strategic guidance that outlines the principles governing stabilization missions and the make-up and processes of the design and management of peace operations with stabilization mandates and tasks.

As can be gathered from the nature of the mandates and the tasks, stabilization operations, apart from the military and security tools, additionally require the use of political and peacebuilding activities simultaneously or incrementally. Peace operations with stabilization mandates and tasks engage in military operations aimed at neutralizing insurgent and terrorist groups and undertake security and rule-of-law tasks to help restore the authority of the state and humanitarian and peacebuilding works for the delivery of humanitarian assistance and for rebuilding social and economic infrastructure. Stabilization operations aim at addressing the immediate security and humanitarian needs of the affected society and creating conditions for the restoration of peace and security.

By their very nature stabilization operations are multidimensional. They involve the use of military, police and civilian instruments to address the security, socio-economic, humanitarian and political ills underlying the insecurity and violence in conflict-affected societies. Military instruments are used to support host society security forces to create the initial security conditions. This is done through security operations aimed at eliminating, deterring or controlling violent armed elements. Police and civilian instruments are deployed to enforce order, rebuild the rule of law and security institutions and assist in efforts to deliver humanitarian assistance and reconstruct administrative and public service infrastructure.

Clearly, integrated design and planning is key for peace operations with stabilization mandates. The military and security components should be designed and planned together with the political, diplomatic, economic recovery and humanitarian dimensions. These different elements should be deployed together, and as such the military and security personnel should work closely with the head of mission, the chief of the police and other civilian counterparts to establish appropriate structures and processes that will facilitate a shared understanding, integrated design and planning, and coordinated execution and assessment.

The AU's experience with stabilization mandates and missions

The AU's experience with stabilization mandates and missions started when it deployed its now long-running and biggest mission to Somalia. Although the African Union Mission in Somalia (AMISOM) was conceived to facilitate the withdrawal of Ethiopian troops and as a gap-filling measure in 2007 (Dersso 2010a), due regard was given to the prevailing security and governance issues in Somalia. Accordingly, as well as al-Shabaab's military campaign against Somalia's nominal government, the Transitional Federal Government (TFG),

AMISOM's mandate was from the outset cognizant of the destruction of government institutions responsible for provision of security and other public services and for maintaining law and order. When the Peace and Security Council (PSC) authorized the deployment of AMISOM, it mandated the mission (i) to provide support to the Transitional Federal Institutions (TFIs) in their efforts to stabilize the situation in the country and further dialogue and reconciliation, (ii) to facilitate the provision of humanitarian assistance, and (iii) to create conducive conditions for long-term stabilization, reconstruction and development in Somalia (African Union 2007).

Within the framework of these mandates, AMISOM is entrusted with carrying out the following tasks:

- supporting dialogue and reconciliation in Somalia, working with all stakeholders;
- providing, as appropriate, protection to the TFIs and their key infrastructure, to enable them to carry out their functions;
- assisting in the implementation of the National Security and Stabilization Plan of Somalia, particularly the effective reestablishment and training of all relevant Somali security forces, bearing in mind the programmes already being implemented by some of Somalia's bilateral and multilateral partners;
- providing, within capabilities and as appropriate, technical and other support to the disarmament and stabilization efforts;
- monitoring, in areas of deployment of its forces, the security situation;
- facilitating, as may be required and within capabilities, humanitarian operations, including the repatriation and reintegration of refugees and the resettlement of IDPs;
- protecting its personnel, installations and equipment, with the right to self-defence. (Ibid.)

As is clear from the terms of AMISOM's mandate (covering a range of stabilization objectives) and the details of the task assigned to it (support for reconciliation, implementation of the stabilization plan, including the re-estab-lishment of all security forces, disarmament and stabilization efforts), AMISOM was from the very beginning framed as a stabilization operation. Seen in this light, it is the first AU mission with a stabilization mandate and relevant tasks. But the force size and design of AMISOM was such that until 2011 it operated mainly as a military operation focusing almost exclusively on defending itself, the TFG institutions and key infrastructures in Mogadishu (Dersso 2010b). It was only after its force size was expanded and its mandate was further enriched that AMISOM started to undertake more robustly stabilization tasks involving combat operations and the reclaiming of territories in al-Shabaab's control.

With AMISOM registering success in pushing al-Shabaab from many areas under its control, the need for increasing stabilization activities and diversifying the design and composition of AMISOM became evident. In this context, the AU expanded the deployment of the police component of AMISOM. Additionally, AMISOM, despite continuing to be military-heavy in its structure, started to undertake further stabilization tasks. Such tasks included supporting the re-establishment of local/regional administration in areas liberated from al-Shabaab, the training and rebuilding of Somali security forces, and assisting in the enforcement of law and order and in the provision of humanitarian assistance. In this context, the mission's police component became particularly important. Its mandate required the police component to help train, mentor and advise the Somali Police Force (SPF), although AMISOM's Formed Police Units have the additional task of public order management. The mission is also mandated to help facilitate humanitarian relief and civil–military operations.

With the resurgence of African peace operations in the past three years, stabilization mandates and operations have become common features of African peace operations. Such has been the case with respect to both AFISMA and MISCA. AFISMA's mandate has thus been multidimensional in scope. Accordingly, the objectives AFISMA was assigned included (i) ensuring the security of the transitional institutions; (ii) restructuring and reorganizing the Malian security and defence forces (MDSF); and (iii) restoring state authority over the northern part of Mali and combating terrorist and criminal networks. On its deployment, AFISMA was thus involved in securing and stabilizing the northern territories recovered from armed militant groups and thereby enabling the Malian authorities to regain and consolidate their control over northern Mali.

When deciding on the deployment of MISCA, the PSC authorized MISCA 'to: (i) [undertake] the protection of civilians and the restoration of security and public order, through the implementation of appropriate measures; (ii) the stabilization of the country and the restoration of the authority of the central Government; (iii) the reform and restructuring of the defense and security sector; and (iv) the creation of conditions conducive for the provision of humanitarian assistance to population in need' (African Union 2013a). It is interesting to note that in a development that registered significant improvement on AMISOM, particularly from the perspective of stabilization operations which call for multidimensional elements, MISCA's force composition was initially a total strength of 3,652, including 3,500 uniformed personnel (2,475 for the military component and 1,025 for the police component) and 152 civilians.

Despite the fact that African peace operations reflect clear recognition at the strategic levels of the need for stabilization operations, and recent operations have been assigned stabilization mandates, the design and composition of the missions, as well as the resources and logistics made available, have made the missions in almost all cases ill equipped to undertake and support stabilization activities. The experience of AMISOM in particular is instructive. In this regard, five major issues can be identified. First, AMISOM was designed and implemented as a military-heavy undertaking. As subsequent missions also show, AU missions like AMISOM, with their military-heavy character, seem to be more suited to undertaking military operations than the full spectrum of stabilization activities.

Secondly, AMISOM was not optimally configured to support the stabilization of Somalia. Its police and civilian components were initially absent and to date remain woefully inadequate, not only in size but also in their technical expertise for implementing effective stabilization activities. Akpasom and Lotze thus rightly noted that '[w]hilst a limited police presence, and an even smaller civilian component, have been established in Mogadishu, the mission is still not adequately designed to provide support to stabilization processes once military operations have been concluded' (2014: 18, 23).

Thirdly, AMISOM has not been provided with the required resources and capabilities, in terms of the composition of its personnel, availability of specialist expertise, provision of logistics and necessary funding. These are challenges that AMISOM shares with both AFISMA and MISCA. Fourthly, 'AMISOM stabilization activities to date have taken place in a relative policy vacuum, operating without sufficient strategic guidance from the AU Commission on how it is to approach and prioritize its stabilization mandate and activities' (ibid.: 24).

Finally, AMISOM and similar AU operations have not been adequately linked to effective political efforts to resolve the conflicts. Indeed, for many years, AMISOM has been operating in the absence of any meaningful political process. In 2010, it was accordingly observed that, like any similar peace operations that are not by their design fit to resolve a conflict, 'the use of AMISOM (alone and in the absence of a political framework/process) has proven to be utterly inadequate for the task of stabilizing the security situation in Somalia' (Dersso 2010a: 14).

The security environment that necessitated stabilization mandates and missions in Africa

Although it was not the only place where the shift in the nature of conflicts from interstate to intra-state conflicts decidedly shaped the redefinition of the role of UN peacekeeping during the post-Cold War period, it was in response to this shift in the African context that traditional UN peacekeeping (designed for interstate conflicts) was reformulated and made to adapt to address intra-state conflict situations. Today, we are once again witnessing changes in the nature of the context in which peacekeeping operations are being undertaken. Unlike in the 1990s, traditional rebel groups are increasingly becoming rare and in their place a diverse multiplicity of factionalized militant armed groups have emerged. Much of the threat to peace and security in Africa today arises from insurgency, acts of terrorism and the proliferation of militia groups and organized criminal networks operating in fragile and conflict zones.

The environments in which African peace operations are deployed today are characterized by both the sheer complexity of issues and the multiplicity of groups involved. Apart from regular government forces and a declining number of traditional armed rebel groups, other actors that are becoming prominent include irregular groups, by which we mean clan militias, guerrilla forces, criminal networks, religious or ethnic militia groups and terrorist groups, as well as mercenaries and warlords. Unlike intra-state conflicts involving clearly identifiable rebel groups and conventional warfare, in these complex environments conflicts are not conducted following traditional warfare methods.

The most significant change relates to the modus operandi of armed opposition groups and the means and method of violence. Conflicts increasingly take the form of asymmetric warfare in which hit-and-run guerrilla tactics, the use of increasingly sophisticated improvised explosive devices (IEDs), targeted assassinations, indiscriminate attacks on civilians, suicide and roadside bombings, and sniper fire have become common.

As in the past, in many of these environments the state machinery has collapsed or has been absent. Governance structures such as the security sector, the justice system and public administration, as well as local structures, are dysfunctional or totally non-existent. In other cases, these conflicts themselves lead to the collapse of state institutions and the breakdown of law and order, as the case of the CAR during 2013 has shown. Equally importantly, at the social level, these conflicts also create and entrench divisions and animosity among different sections of society.

The context in which peace operations operate in Africa has thus become one that calls for a multi-pronged approach that combines robust and comprehensive mandates and tasks. These increasingly cover, among other factors, counter-terrorism and counter-insurgency, as well as combat operations to neutralize militant insurgent and terrorist groups, protection of civilians, supporting the building or rebuilding of security and rule-of-law institutions, providing for the rolling out and rebuilding of government administration and social infrastructure, and assisting in national reconciliation and peacebuilding efforts.

The African Standby Force through the prism of stabilization missions

As envisaged in the PSC Protocol, the ASF is to be prepared for rapid deployment for a range of peacekeeping operations (African Union 2002: Article 13(3)), including

- observation and monitoring missions;
- other types of peace operations;
- intervention in accordance with Art. 4(h) and (j) of the Constitutive Act;

- preventive deployment in order to prevent a conflict from escalating, or an ongoing conflict from spreading to neighbouring areas or states, or the resurgence of violence after peace agreements are achieved;
- peacebuilding, including post-conflict disarmament and demobilization; and
- humanitarian assistance in situations of conflicts and major natural disasters.

The ASF is composed of standby multidisciplinary contingents. Accordingly, the Policy Framework for the Establishment of the ASF and the Military Staff Committee (MSC) and the Road Map for the Operationalization of the ASF (Roadmap I) conceived of the ASF as composed of military, police and civilian components.

The multidimensional conception of the ASF makes it suitable for undertaking stabilization operations. Given that the nature of conflict situations on the continent, as pointed out, is complex and calls for a multifaceted approach involving capabilities to address not only the security and the military but also the political, humanitarian, developmental and legal dimensions of the conflicts, the composition of the ASF should accordingly involve all the different required instruments.

As the experience of African peace operations has thus far shown, and the development of the ASF shows, both African peace operations and the ASF suffer from inadequate provision of police and civilian capacities. As the report of the Independent Panel on the Assessment of the ASF observed, despite the steps taken to develop a multidimensional peace operations capability, 'progress has been uneven, and civilian and police capacities have not received as much attention as military capacities' (African Union 2013b).

The Policy Framework for the Establishment of the ASF and the MSC (African Union 2003) identifies six possible conflict and mission scenarios that the ASF is likely to face and will need to respond to.

Scenarios	Description
1	AU/Regional Military Adviser to a political mission
2	AU/Regional Observer Mission co-deployed with UN Mission
3	Stand-alone AU/Regional Observer Mission
4	AU Regional Peacekeeping Force for Chapter VI and preventive deployment missions
5	AU Peacekeeping Force for complex multidimensional peace operation – 'low-level spoilers'
6	AU intervention in cases of grave circumstances

Table 3.1 ASF mission scenarios

Source: Adapted from the Policy Framework for the Establishment of the African Standby Force and the Military Staff Committee, ch. 1, para. 1.6

The experience from African peace operations and the complexity of the operating environment mean that the design and conduct of peace operations does not fit any particular model. Operating in hostile situations where there is no peace to keep and the structure and authority of the state are lacking, peace operations require and tend to use a wide range of military, police and civilian instruments and undertake diverse tasks including monitoring, enforcement, protection of civilians, security, rule of law and governance, humanitarian assistance and human rights. The result is that the scenarios as outlined became outdated, not being in sync with the AU's experience in peace operations and the changes witnessed in the operating environment since the 2000s.

Given that the ASF was originally conceived based on the experience of the UN, and prior to the AU developing experience and empirical knowledge of peace operations, it was formulated and developed to be a consensual peace-keeping instrument. The AU experience in peace operations has additionally revealed that the experience on the ground has overtaken the ASF concept. Africa's peace operations in Somalia, Mali and the CAR involved not only peace enforcement mandates but also active combat operations. As the AU Panel on the Assessment of the ASF has pointed out, there is today a significant gap 'between the consensual peacekeeping model the ASF is designed for, and the actual peace enforcement and stability operations the AU has been called on to undertake in Somalia, Mali and the CAR' (De Coning 2014: 34, 36).

At the level of strategic guidance and doctrinal framework, the ASF concept has reflected very little or no awareness of stabilization missions and tasks. This lack of adequate reflection of the requirements of the operating environment for stabilization activities means that stabilization operations have been undertaken and stabilization mandates are assigned to missions in a doctrinal void. At the level of doctrinal framework, the ASF concept also remains military-heavy. There is thus a need for a more comprehensive approach to articulate an all-encompassing and multidimensional African peace support capability.

Finally, seen through the prism of stabilization missions and the require-ments for the provision of rapid response capability, the ASF has proved to be not well suited to rapid deployment and response. With the failure of African countries to rapidly respond to the emergency that Mali faced in early 2013, and the ASF considered not fit to equip the AU for rapid response (ibid.: 39),[3] the AU took the decision to establish a 'gap-filling' mechanism by way of the ACIRC. Although it is far from certain whether the ACIRC model can deliver the required rapidity, the ACIRC represents a clear recognition that in terms of rapid response there is a need for an alternative model.

Both from the experience of African peace operations and the foregoing brief examination of the ASF concept through the prism of stabilization operations, it emerges that the ASF is clearly in need of some reform or adjustment.

1. Doctrinal clarity At the doctrinal level, the strategic guidance of African peace operations should be reformulated to encompass the complexity of AU missions and the changes and dynamism of the operating environment. Such a reformulation should cover a wide range of operations, including traditional peacekeeping, peace enforcement and stabilization operations. Drawing on the experience of African peace operations, most notably from the long-running AMISOM, this should articulate the essence of stabilization mandates and missions and outline the principles that govern such mandates and operations, including protection of civilians, observance of international humanitarian law and human rights.

Additionally, the AU's doctrine for the ASF needs to become more than a military doctrine. As Gordon (2015) pointed out, '[w]hile the AU does not aspire to replicate the full UN multi-agency, multi-dimensional capability brought to a UN mission, it does recognize that the AU must develop a politically led, integrated capability'. The doctrine should accordingly both be multidimensional in its coverage and give strategic guidance not only to military but also to police and civilian instruments. As the paper pointed out, '[t]his matters if the ASF is to have a capability, which can interoperate with, or hand over to, a UN mission' (ibid.).

It is also crucial that the trend of military deployment as a default position whenever conflicts break out is critically revised. Significantly, the disconnect between military operations and the political efforts to resolve conflicts should be bridged. In other words, the use of military operations should be anchored in a clearly articulated political strategy and process for resolving the conflict or the crisis that led to the deployment of peace operations.

2. Reconsidering the ASF planning scenarios The six deployment scenarios for the ASF were elaborated before the AU accumulated its now relatively rich experience in peace operations. They were based on conflict dynamics prior to 2000. Many of the AU's peace operations were not designed and deployed with reference to the ASF planning scenarios. Indeed, these various operations do not neatly fit into the ASF planning scenarios. This is due not only to the lack of reference to the ASF concept in the deployment of Africa's peace operations thus far, but mainly to the complexity of the operating environment, which has become substantively different from the environment that obtained at the time of the elaboration of the ASF scenarios.

Put simply, the ASF concept as originally articulated did not envisage ASF operations engaging in active combat and offensive operations. Although reference was made to spoilers in scenario 5 ASF operations, this scenario encompassed only what it called low-level 'spoilers'. It did not cover situations in which major 'spoilers' – for example, al-Shabaab or Boko Haram – are involved. It can be fairly assumed that scenario 5, by virtue of its scope, allows the use of force only at a tactical level. In contrast, the AU operations in Somalia, Mali and to some extent in the CAR engaged the use of force at strategic levels.

3. *Rectifying the imbalance in the composition of ASF capabilities* Although there has been increasing attention given to African peace operations and to the development of the ASF to involve increasing levels of police and civilian capabilities, both AU operations and the ASF continue to suffer from serious imbalances in the composition of their capabilities. The experience thus far shows that successful operations require multidimensional and integrated capabilities. Military and security instruments will not succeed in delivering stabilization unless they are accompanied by or used alongside police and civilian capabilities. Police and civilian expertise are thus key for effective implementation of stabilization mandates and the success of stabilization operations.

The imbalance in the composition of AU operations and the development of the ASF with few police and even fewer civilian capabilities need to be rectified. There is a need for higher levels of support for and investment in building police and civilian capabilities. The use of such capabilities is needed not only in conditions where armed violence has been contained but also even in high-intensity operations. In the light of the recent trend of transition of AU missions into UN missions, rectifying the imbalance through higher investment in building police and civilian capabilities will ensure smooth and interoperable transitions.

4. *The provision of resources and logistics* AU missions suffer from a shortage of the required resources, including for training, equipment and logistics support. AU member states lack the expertise and equipment required to undertake specialized tasks, including combat engineering, logistics resupply, medical support and vehicle maintenance. These problems facing African peace operations generally affect the implementation of stabilization mandates and the conduct of stabilization operations. In the context of Somalia, for example, Paul Williams noted that, for the AU, stabilization in Somalia refers to the multi-dimensional process of extending the administrative authority of the federal government, delivering services – including food and water, healthcare, shelter, policing and de-mining – to local populations and conducting a programme of disarmament, demobilization and reintegration of al-Shabaab and other militias that wish to lay down their arms. Yet, he stated, outside Mogadishu,

'AMISOM is hobbled by numbers of troops and police that are insufficient to stabilise its large area of operations' (Williams 2012: 34). Even with more troop surges in 2013/14, AMISOM continues to face critical shortages in supplies of equipment, logistics and enablers. These shortages have affected and still affect the ability of AMISOM to deliver effectively in its stabilization role. We thus agrees with Akpasom and Lotze that 'where stabilization mandates have been provided to operations, the appropriate resources should be provided to missions to implement these mandates, and the appropriate capabilities should be developed for the implementation of such mandates'(Akpasom and Lotze 2014: 25).

5. *Rapid response capability* Given that the trend of conflicts and security threats demands deploying rapid, robust and agile interventions, it is doubtful if the ASF, made up of contributions from all member states, organized into five regional standby forces and involving time-consuming multilevel decision-making procedure, is suitable for undertaking such operations. In the light of the experience from various African peace operations, and recent challenges faced in deploying a rapid intervention force as in Mali, the ASF policy frame-work should be reviewed. As the experience in Mali and the deployment of the Force Intervention Brigade with an explicit offensive mandate within the United Nations Organization Stabilization Mission in the Democratic Republic of the Congo (MONUSCO) attested, Article 4(h) situations involving the risk or occurrence of mass-atrocity crimes are not the only situations requiring rapid response capability. Rapid response capability is also required to respond to emergency situations that arise in a country or in an operating environment owing to violent acts of hostile insurgent or terrorist groups.

6. *Coordination* Stabilization mandates and operations require the integrated application and use of a wide range of tools drawing on and harnessing the contribution of a variety of actors, including, apart from the diverse mission components, other multilateral actors, humanitarian actors and available national actors in the host society. Planning for and institutionalizing processes and mechanisms for strategic and operational coordination are key to a successful and comprehensive execution of stabilization mandates.

Conclusion

This chapter discussed the evolution of changes in the nature of mandates and tasks that African peace operations are assigned and called on to perform. In this context, it briefly analysed the emerging trend in African peace operations of the use of stabilization mandates and operations. Against the background of the AU's experience in stabilization mandates and operations, and an overview of what stabilization mandates and operations entail, the chapter scrutinized the ASF concept and the process for its operational readiness through the prism of stabilization mandates and operations. This allowed us to cast a spotlight on areas of the ASF concept that require change, refinement or adjustment, informed by the empirical evidence of the AU's initial experience of stabilization missions.

It is hoped that this chapter will serve as a basis to examine and fully address the following and related questions: What is the experience of the AU with stabilization mandates and operations? What led to the increasing assignment of stabilization mandates and tasks to African peace operations? What do stabilization missions and mandates involve? What do stabilization mandates entail in terms of the design and composition of the mission, the expertise and tools required for such a mission and the resource and logistics provision for the mission? Are stabilization activities anticipated and properly reflected in the ASF concept? What changes, if any, do stabilization mandates and operations entail for the ASF? How should such changes or adjustments be made?

Notes

1 Exercise AMANI Africa II, conducted to review the operational readiness of the ASF for 2015, was held in November 2014.

2 See generally United States Government (2011).

3 As De Coning observed, 'the standing readiness dimension of the ASF concept has not and is unlikely to be used as assumed in the design of the ASF'.

References

African Union (2002) *Protocol Relating to the Establishment of the Peace and Security Council of the African Union*, Durban: African Union, www.peaceau. org/uploads/psc-protocol-en.pdf, accessed 18 November 2015.

— (2003) *Policy Framework for the Establishment of the African Standby Force and the Military Staff Committee*, Addis Ababa: African Union.

— (2007) *PSC/PR/Comm(LXIX): Communiqué of the 69th meeting of the Peace and Security Council*, Addis Ababa: African Union, www. ausitroom-psd.org/Documents/ PSC2007/69th/Communique/ CommuniqueEng.pdf, accessed 18 November 2015.

— (2013a) *PSC/PR/Comm(CCCLXXXV): Communiqué*, Addis Ababa: African Union, www.peaceau.org/uploads/psc-com-385-car-19-07-2013.pdf, accessed 18 November 2015.

— (2013b) *Report of the Independent Panel of Experts, Assessment of the African Standby Force and Plan of Action for achieving full operational capability by 2015*, Addis Ababa: African Union, Unpublished.

Akpasom, Y. and W. Lotze (2014) 'The shift to stabilization operations: considerations for African peace support operations', *Conflict Trends*, 2: 2–56.

De Coning, C. (2014) 'Enhancing the efficiency of the ASF: the case for a shift to a just-in-time rapid response model', *Conflict Trends*, 2: 34–40.

Dersso, S. A. (2010a) 'Somalia dilemmas: changing security dynamics, limited policy options', ISS Paper no. 218, Addis Ababa: Institute for Security Studies, www.issafrica.org/uploads/ Paper218.pdf, accessed 18 November 2015.

— (2010b) 'The role and place of the ASF within the African Peace and Security Architecture', ISS Paper no. 209, Addis Ababa: Institute for Security Studies, www.issafrica. org/uploads/209.pdf, accessed 18 November 2015.

Gordon, R. (2015) *A comparative on doctrines and principles for multidimensional peace operations: a case for harmonized and enhanced interoperability*, International Forum for the Challenges of Peace Operations, www. marshallarmyrotc.org/documents/ GordonStudyonDocandPriniples1.pdf, accessed 18 November 2015.

Karlsrud, J. (2015) 'The UN at war: examining the consequences of peace enforcement mandates for the UN peacekeeping operations in the CAR, the DRC and Mali', *Third World Quarterly*, XXXVI(1): 40–54.

United States Government (2011) *Joint Publication 3-07: Stability Operations*, United States Government, www.dtic. mil/doctrine/new_pubs/jp3_07.pdf, accessed 18 November 2015.

Williams, P. D. (2012) 'AMISOM', *RUSI Journal*, CLVII(5): 32–45.

4 | The relationship between the AU and the RECs/RMs in relation to peace and security in Africa: subsidiarity and inevitable common destiny

Michelle Ndiaye

Introduction

The relationship between the AU and the RECs/RMs has over the years been recognized as central to the APSA. The concept of subsidiarity is often regarded as its nearly sacrosanct foundational principle. But at the same time, a too-principled approach to subsidiarity may have become a real stumbling block in terms of providing strategic and timely responses to crisis situations in Africa. This has been especially visible with regard to peace operations. A reinterpretation and realignment to the AU's evolving peace operations doctrine, as well as a definition of its context-driven practicality, is required. The capability of the AU to mandate, mount and conduct peace operations should not be held hostage by the discussion on what subsidiarity means for the overall relationship between the AU and the RECs/RMs. Recent developments suggest that the principle of subsidiarity is, in practice, often seen as only one of several considerations for defining mission-specific partnerships. This is particularly true for AU–UN mission partnerships, and may increasingly be relevant for AU–REC/RM partnerships in missions.

The chapter first situates subsidiarity in the legal framework of the APSA. It then discusses how this principle is applied in practice in mission-specific contexts, focusing on four key issues: political will, operational competence, legal authority and finance. Procedural constraints, for example, determine the capacity of the AU, the RECs and member states to respond to crises and, therefore, need equal attention.

I argue that while the concept is important, in practice the intra-regional political objectives and the practicalities of actually deploying peace operations matter more. Interlocking and flexible models for institutional relations between the AU and the RECs/RMs, and also among RECs/RMs themselves, are needed because the requirements of peace operations will continue to pull these institutions into various arrangements for collaboration. These developments will require the pragmatic evolution of mandates and modes of operation of peace operations towards a more diverse and less hierarchical approach.

When the African Peace and Security Architecture was created, the relationship between institutions at the continental and at the regional level was established as a hierarchical one (African Union 2002).[1] To the extent that this issue is reflected at all, there is a clear political commitment that institutions and mandates at the continental level shall supersede national and subregional ones.

The Protocol Establishing the Peace and Security Council is a component of the legal framework of the APSA. It had been adopted already at the First Ordinary Session of the Assembly of the African Union, in July 2002. It mandates the AU to promote peace in Africa mainly through the Peace and Security Council (PSC). Article 7 of the Protocol states the many and wide powers of the PSC in eighteen clauses, which puts it at the centre of policy-making on African peace and security. The PSC shall exercise these powers 'in conjunction with the Chairperson of the Commission'. Where intervention in a member state may be required, the PSC will act upon a decision by the Assembly (e). Member states summarily agree that 'the PSC acts on their behalf' (ibid.: Article 7.2).

The RECs are mentioned only to the extent that the PSC has the power to 'promote close harmonization, co-ordination and co-operation between Regional Mechanisms and the Union in the promotion and maintenance of peace, security and stability in Africa' (ibid.: Article 7.1.e).[2]

The Common African Defence and Security Policy (CADSP), adopted in 2004, highlights the need for cooperation between the AU and the RECs/RMs. In this, it recommends a 'coordination role' for the AU Peace and Security Council.

A more nuanced approach, deviating from a simply hierarchical understanding of the relationship between the AU and the RECs, was introduced with the 2008 Memorandum of Understanding (MoU) between the AU and the RECs/RMs in the area of peace and security. It postulates the need for 'adherence to the principles of subsidiarity, complementarity and comparative advantage, in order to optimize the partnership between the Union, the RECs and the Coordinating Mechanisms'. More specifically, Article XX of the MoU states:

> Without prejudice to the primary role of the Union in the promotion and maintenance of peace, security and stability in Africa, the RECs and, where appropriate, the Coordinating Mechanisms shall be encouraged to anticipate and prevent conflicts within and among their Member States and, where conflicts do occur, to undertake peace-making and peace-building efforts to resolve them, including the deployment of peace support missions. (African Union 2008)

What does that mean? The principle of subsidiarity states that in a hierarchically organized political or administrative system, tasks should preferably be handled by the lowest level on which an adequate result can be achieved.

Hierarchy is moderated in that the lower levels are given a role and rights to act. They own a particular space in which the respective higher level may not directly interfere. However, the lower levels are still bound to act in congruence with the objectives and principles of the higher ones.

Subsidiarity gives recognition to the fact that in governance systems lower levels may enjoy stronger political legitimacy because they are closer to the citizens. This is an important issue for the African Union, which is concerned with the issue of legitimacy and pursues a conscious agenda of connecting to the 'African people'.

But a straightforward interpretation and application of the principle is not possible. The AU PSC Protocol, the CADSP and the MoU have slightly different wordings, leaving open many possible interpretations. Moreover, the establishment of most RECs – and usually with a mandate to deal with peace and security issues in their respective regions – precedes that of the PSC. ECOWAS and SADC especially see themselves as incumbents, having, through long political processes as well as action on the ground, established themselves as key security actors in their respective regions, sometimes long before the emergence of the African Union.

ECOWAS was created in 1975, with a focus on economic development and integration (as its name suggests). In 1981, its member states signed the ECOWAS Mutual Defence Treaty, which also foresaw the establishment of security coordination and intervention mechanisms. This did not take place, however (Hutchful 1999).

Notwithstanding an apparent lack of mandate and dedicated mechanisms, ECOWAS mounted the first African peace operation, ECOMOG (the ECOWAS Ceasefire Monitoring Group), in July 1990. This was only about six months after the breakout of the Liberian civil war. Nigerian leadership in every aspect played a decisive role. ECOMOG also set the precedent for a distinct feature of African peace operations: their enforcement mandate and political staying power. This came at the cost of neutrality. Whether ECOMOG was successful as a military intervention is hotly debated (Usman-Janguza 2014). Nevertheless, it was redeployed to Sierra Leone (1997), Guinea-Bissau (1998), Ivory Coast (2003) and eventually again to Liberia (2003), again with mixed success. It was actually long after the first ECOMOG, and upon drawing lessons from it, that the ECOWAS Mechanism for Conflict Prevention, Management and Resolution, Peacekeeping and Security was established in 1999. But this was still way ahead of the PSC Protocol.

SADC was established in 1992; in the struggle against South Africa's apartheid regime, security had always been one of its preoccupations. Post-apartheid, and with new security challenges to be faced, in 2001 the SADC Treaty was amended to create the Organ on Politics, Defence and Security Cooperation. SADC did not, however, build a similar reputation in peace operations.

South Africa and Botswana mounted a peace operation in 1998/99 to Lesotho, claiming it was a SADC humanitarian peacekeeping mission, but without support from the SADC summit (Likoti 2007). Several SADC members also dispatched a peacekeeping force to the DRC in 1998. Its intervention subsequently fell apart, however, as it was politically disunited because two of its member states, Zimbabwe and Angola, were directly involved in the conflict – but against the will of South Africa as its largest and strongest member (see, e.g., Ngoma 2004).

African Union and the RECs in mediating security crises

The PSC has, gradually, assumed the pivotal role in managing peace and security on the continent. This is particularly true for political mediation and the application of sanction regimes. In some of these cases, the PSC has intervened in crises, assuming a lead role that could in principle have been handled by the RECs. In these cases, the higher political profile of the AU, as well as political impasses at the REC level, has been decisive in bolstering AU involvement. But there are also instances where the AU sought a role for itself, but was eventually denied such a role by the concerned RECs.

During the post-electoral crisis in Kenya in early 2008, among other international efforts for mediation the AU quickly gained a prominent role, endorsing a High-level Panel of Eminent Personalities led by Kofi Annan. The panel was successful in mediating the crisis, based on the weight of the personalities involved. The concerned REC – the Intergovernmental Authority on Development (IGAD) – was never involved.

During the Madagascar crisis beginning in 2009, the AU appointed a Special Envoy, Ablassé Ouedraogo; however, SADC's mediator, Joaquim Chissano, became the effective leader of the international mediation effort (Ancas 2011). In the DRC crisis, as in Kenya, the involvement of the concerned REC – in this case ECCAS – was never an option, whereas the AU intervened based on its political weight. A similar situation was found with regard to the Arab awakening and subsequent violence, where in operational terms the northern African community of states NARC was among the victims and the AU PSC was the relevant decision-making body in the Libya crisis.

When the security crisis in the western Sahel escalated, there were initiatives by both the concerned REC – here ECOWAS – and the AU towards mediating the conflict. In this case, the AU appointed former president Pierre Buyoya first as its High Representative for Mali and the Sahel and later as head of the African-led International Support Mission in Mali (AFISMA). The diplomatic initiative by ECOWAS was hampered by the fact that some of the countries involved, notably Algeria and Mauritania, are not part of ECOWAS.

There are some lessons to be drawn from these examples of 'subsidiarity' in action in the diplomatic field. Proximity often plays an important role, because a security crisis in a given country will affect neighbours directly, giving them more often a strong reason to intervene. But when there is a strong reason for the AU to get involved, it may prevail even if a REC feels uneasy about it. Southern Africa may provide the exception to this rule, where there is an instinct among its leaders to 'close up' and not expose internal division. Some conflicts are large enough to draw in the UN. In such cases, it is the AU rather than the REC that will be expected to represent the African element, as a body with more political weight.

Subsidiarity and peace operations

A closer look at past experience allows us to identify four key tensions linked to the issue of subsidiarity that contribute to shaping African-led peace operations. 'Political will' and 'operational competence' will usually speak for a bottom-up approach to mounting peace operations, whereas 'legal authority' and 'finance' will usually drive a more top-down approach.

Political will Mounting a peace operation requires strong political commitment – especially when the operation may involve combat and fatalities. In quite a number of cases the commitment must also be sustained over years, while little or no progress may be recorded on the ground. ECOMOG and AMISOM are examples of missions where neighbours play or played an important role in mounting and sustaining effective missions, although not necessarily through the respective RECs. The United Nations Interim Security Force for Abyei (UNISFA) is another example where a neighbour was ready and capable of providing troops and logistics because vital interests were seen as being at stake.

Operational competence Similarly, shorter distances and knowledge of the terrain favour the involvement of neighbours and a bottom-up approach to mounting peace operations in general. Tactics and logistics are much easier to handle for neighbours – indeed, most peace operations demonstrate the tactical and logistics advantages of involving neighbours as well as the tactical and logistics challenges of involving troops from afar. Also, strengthening operational competence by virtue of a bottom-up approach makes sense when seen against the African Union's quest for African-led solutions, which are expected to be better informed about and better attuned to the realities on the ground than operations that are mounted from afar. This argument is based on the widely held and very plausible notion that each violent conflict is unique, and that dealing with it needs familiarity with local conditions and contact with the specific actors on the ground. These are the arguments that propo-nents of an AU intervention capacity use, at a different level, in comparing AU-mandated and UNSC-mandated peace operations. Moreover, this view is backed by the practical experience of ECOWAS' intervention in the Liberian civil war, widely seen as an example of African vigour and the 'doability' of deploying in less than optimal situations. Here, the political commitment was clear, and resources could be raised within the region. Possibly, the IGAD-led intervention in Somalia may also count in this regard.

In contrast, critical military capabilities – mainly surveillance and air transport – are often beyond the means of neighbours and the RECs. To acquire them will need involving higher levels, or distant yet capable states as sponsors.

Legal authority and political legitimacy The legal regime for peace operations is quite inconsistent, and the prospects of streamlining it through adjusting international legal instruments are possibly not very good. Some RECs at least nominally retain the right to mount peace operations without the approval of the AU level; for example, SADC and ECOWAS.[3] However, the 2005 *Roadmap for the Operationalization of the African Standby Force* explicitly states: 'The AU will seek UN Security Council authorization of its enforcements actions. Similarly, the [RECs] will seek AU authorization of their interventions' (African Union 2005).

Originally it was thought that the 2008 MoU between the AU and the RECs/RMs would be followed up by detailed arrangements regarding the individual pillars of the African Peace and Security Architecture, among them the ASF. However, this has not happened. At the highest level, the authority of the AU PSC to mount peace operations has been contested on the grounds of Chapter VIII of the UN Charter, which is being interpreted differently by various 'P5' states,[4] some UN representatives and the AU.

Against this background, there appears to be emerging an understanding that the UN Security Council (UNSC) will 'no longer authorize an African REC/RM to undertake a peace operation, like it did with ECOMOG and ECOMIL in the past, without the consent and authority of the AU Peace and Security Council' (De Coning et al. 2015).

Financing A key determining factor, as so often, is the financial ability of Africa to pay for peace operations. Here, it has become abundantly clear that only UN funds are large enough to mount or sustain sizeable peace operations and that the UN – and more specifically the P5 – are not ready to relinquish their funding authority. Hence, UN legal authorization is a precondition for UN financing of peace operations.

These four key notions will now be exemplified with regard to the Somalia, Mali and Boko Haram crises.

The case of AMISOM

Both IGAD and the AU had been working in conjunction on the Somalia crisis (Mays 2009). In 2004, there appeared to be an opportunity to consolidate peace with the establishment of the Transitional Federal Government. Upon the request of the AU PSC in early 2005, IGAD worked out a plan to support the TFG, including the deployment of an international peace operation called IGASOM. This was endorsed in September 2006 by the PSC. However, IGASOM failed to deploy and the IGAD's efforts were frustrated. Of course, there were many reasons for this. Some of them are relevant to our discussion.

First, IGAD, as the 'concerned' REC – and mandated as such in early 2005 by the AU PSC to design the international intervention – was perceived as biased by the Somali actors. Thus, IGAD came up with a plan for an IGAD peace operation, IGASOM. While the rebels – at the time the ICU (Islamic Courts Union) – were totally against any foreign intervention, the Transitional Federal Government opposed any intervention by neighbouring states. This issue was resolved when the plan for the intervention force was changed accordingly, which meant requesting troops from African countries outside of IGAD. With this decision (December 2006/January 2007) the only option was for the AU to assume the responsibility for this operation, and IGASOM became AMISOM. The AU managed to balance regional and African-wide representation, by initially deploying mainly Ugandan (Uganda is an IGAD member) and Burundian troops.[5]

Secondly, other key actors in the Somali crises were the UNSC and the United States, both with their particular agendas and concerns. They were not happy with the initial plans for IGASOM and, under the influence of the USA (among others), the UNSC refused to lift the arms embargo or to underwrite any costs of the peace operation. A middle ground was eventually found for one of the issues – the arms embargo was lifted in December 2006 to allow in principle for an IGASOM deployment. But financing was available only for a truly African force which would not include Ethiopian and Kenyan components. To some extent, IGAD lacked the expertise, capability and clout to lead the negotiations with the global behemoths UNSC and the USA, which were, however, needed to provide the required technical and financial resources.

But IGAD's involvement may still have made a difference. It was possibly instrumental in raising the issue at all. Uganda, Kenya and Ethiopia were deeply concerned about the developments in Somalia and through IGAD and the proposal for IGASOM found a way to express and partially coordinate their political agendas. IGAD can, in this regard, be seen as the breeding ground for AMISOM. Moreover, Uganda, as the main troop-contributing country in the early stages of AMISOM, had a keen security interest in Somalia in that the al-Shabaab terrorists were also active on its soil. Hence, the involvement of neighbours – which eventually was extended to include Kenya and Ethiopia – may at least partly explain AMISOM's political and military staying power in the face of sometimes heavy losses.

Political will for an intervention was strong at all levels, from neighbours and IGAD through the AU PSC up to the UN. But it needed alignment, whereby the level with the required financial resources – the UNSC – prevailed, and the AU was indeed required to make IGAD's case to the UN. Operational competence played an important role in that both IGAD and the AU had to rely on external partners. In legal terms, the UN again prevailed against IGAD on the issue of the arms embargo, but the AU was somehow able to mediate this issue.

The case of Mali

The immediate Mali crisis started as a political one – related to the military coup against an elected government in March 2012. ECOWAS, as the concerned REC, quickly responded with sanctions and a mediation effort, and by developing plans for a peace operation to be called MICEMA. In August, a government of national unity was formed, but was unable to halt the unfolding crisis. Non-ECOWAS members Algeria and Mauritania, meanwhile, were not ready to agree on the ECOWAS peace operation, and neither was the government in Bamako. Because of the fact that non-ECOWAS states were involved, and in the face of divisions within ECOWAS, the AU became more active in mediating the security dimension of the crisis. In the light of a deteriorating security situation, the opponents of an external operation softened their stance and the AU PSC in November decided to deploy an African peace operation, AFISMA.[6] Before that mission could deploy, the rebels' advance on Bamako prompted the Malian government to call upon France for help. France quickly deployed troops in Operation Serval and with the help of Chad restored control of the northern territories. AFISMA started to deploy in April 2013, but already in June 2013 it was rebranded and re-hatted to become the UN-led MINUSMA.

As in the case of AMISOM, the concerned REC was strongly involved in the early stages of crisis management. However, and against prior expectation, ECOWAS was found not able to mount the peace operation, not even with the AU as strategic HQ. Rather, the AU had to take on the planning role, but with support from officers from ECOWAS and the TCCs from the region that had the local knowledge. Equally important, with more international actors being involved and the issues of finance and international law to be addressed, the AU found its role in shaping and representing an 'African' position vis-à-vis the UN. This was a difficult and ambiguous process, particularly in view of the fact that ECOWAS had earlier had direct access to the UNSC. After some hand-wringing, the UNSC also changed its position in this respect and informed ECOWAS that it should direct its requests via Addis Ababa. So in this crisis the hierarchical relationship was being reinforced. At the same time, the political process made only minimal progress. The UN, the AU and

ECOWAS were all unable to influence changes of position, clearly showing the limits of international mediation and the problems of giving a peace operation a 'mediations' mandate. Algeria, which has always been a primary power in the northern Sahel, has re-emerged as an important promoter of peace talks.

Political disunity at REC level – mirroring *inter alia* the conflict within Mali – was and remains an overarching problem. Legality played out as in Somalia, in giving the UNSC the overall say. Operational capability was critical in that the planned ECOWAS mission was widely believed to be incapable, a view which was supported by the fact that there was only one African state – Chad – able to make a difference on the ground. The 'transition' from MICEMA to AFISMA and MINUSMA was strongly shaped by situational regional politics, capabilities and interests (Théroux-Bénoni 2013).

The 'Boko Haram' mission

The creation, in January 2015, of the Multinational Joint Task Force[7] to deal with the Boko Haram threat has so far been an example of flexible and innovative collaboration between member states (Nigeria, Chad, Cameroon, Niger and Benin) and between the RECs (ECOWAS and ECCAS) that grew out of necessity and pragmatism. The Boko Haram problem had for a long time been seen as an internal Nigerian issue, as much by herself as by her neighbours. In early 2013, the organization started to commit its terror attacks also in Cameroon, and it became evident that Niger and Cameroon were being used as staging posts for its operations. Moreover, Nigeria's own attempt at dealing with the problem was unsuccessful. In 2014, Boko Haram was in control of up to 50,000 square kilometres[2] of land and in 2015 it pledged its allegiance to the Islamic state.

If we now look at this case through the lens of our four key issues presented above, the following picture emerges. The political will to deal with the problem was vested in the above-mentioned states, which were also willing to put their own money behind military operations. In fact, Nigeria has officially pledged billions of US dollars of its own money to beefing up its military in the fighting against Boko Haram.[9] The operational requirement to deploy across borders was clear, and was matched especially by Chad's ability to deploy on Nigerian territory. Legal authority for an operation across borders had thus already been granted on a bilateral basis. Here was a typical 'coalition of the willing'. The very purpose of establishing the Multinational Joint Task Force was, hence, to provide political legitimacy and a proper diplomatic framework to the military operation and to eventually access extra money and additional operational capacity for it. These would be mobilized from the international community as well as from other member states. A respective resolution was presented to the UNSC in March 2015, based on the AU decision in January.

The RECs involved, ECOWAS and ECCAS, where thus in a role that they could more comfortably play: rather than being at the forefront of the operation, they would help to establish its political and institutional framework. This was epitomized by the fact that on his 'historic' visit to discuss ECCAS–ECOWAS cooperation with ECOWAS chair Mahama, the president of Ghana, Idriss Déby Itno, as the leader of ECCAS, first made a stopover in Abuja. It also surely helped that ECOWAS members didn't want to once again present an image of weakness, as in the case of Mali and AFISMA. The AU, in this case, played its important role rather in the background – the PSC duly sanctioned ECOWAS and ECCAS decisions without questioning these initiatives or seeking a prominent role for itself, thus paving the way for global recognition. The fact that more than one REC would be involved could have provided a reason for the mission to be AU-hatted. But the ECOWAS–ECCAS horizontal collaboration is a perfect example of giving the 'lower levels' the right to act for themselves without undue interference by the 'centre'. With an operation firmly driven by member states, which then involve the RECs and through them the AU, subsidiarity was adhered to without becoming a constraint. The key was flexibility and pragmatism.

Ahead of the planned deployment of a Multinational Joint Task Force to deal with the Boko Haram threat, Chad, Cameroon, Niger and Nigeria have formed a military alliance to combat these militants, who are fighting to create a hardline Islamic state.

Processes and procedures

Another dimension that shapes the partnership between the AU and the RECs – and indeed the UN – in African peace operations comprises the processes and procedures involved. Peace operations are extremely complex undertakings, confronting institutions that are based on predictability, planning and routine with a situation of uncertainty, fluidity and the requirement for a flexible and rapid response. The ability of peace operations to adapt to these challenges plays an enormous role in their potential effectiveness. Given an improving record of deployment, all is not lost:

> The ... transitions from MICOPAX, the mission of the Economic
> Community of Central African States (ECCAS), to the African Support
> Mission in Central Africa Republic (MISCA), the AU mission, in December
> 2013, followed approximately six months later by the transition from MISCA
> to the UN Multidimensional Integrated Stabilization Mission in the CAR
> (MINUSCA), reflected a significant improvement and showed how quickly
> the UN, AU and RECs learn from previous experiences and adapt to new
> realities. (De Coning et al. 2015)

At the same time, the experience of ECOWAS can be taken as a warning. For Mali, ECOWAS was clearly not able to raise a mission – and the vagueness of its mandate may have been only one of the reasons. Moreover, when this problem became clear, there was no mechanism to establish this very inability and thereby escalate the responsibility to the AU PSC.[10] And because of the lack of a clear mandate from ECOWAS the AU's response was also hobbled. This ushered in a widespread agreement that only the UN would be able to save the situation.

The problem was that according to the principle of subsidiarity, the lower level was not able to 'handle the challenge', but there was no way to establish this fact and hence subsidiarity didn't work in its aspect of upward delegation. Subsidiarity, in this case, became a stumbling block.

It appears that a critical factor in applying subsidiarity in peace operations will be to establish precisely such mechanisms that allow monitoring of whether a REC as the first point of call is capable of handling a situation or not, and then escalating the issue if and when required. This will require open and assertive discussions at the PSC level from day one of an emergency.

Political mediation, peace operations and subsidiarity

Most peace operations in Africa suffer from the fact that – despite their numerous challenges – gains towards stabilization in the military sphere often do not translate into stabilization in the political sphere. But peace operations do not bring peace, not even in a minimalist interpretation. Peace can result only from political processes. Peace operations and political intervention – mediation in AU language – need to go hand in hand.

We can now apply this thought to the issue of subsidiarity. Looking at our examples, we find that political processes are often more viable if they involve neighbours and are directed by the RECs, rather than by the AU or the UN, which are even more distanced from the situation. If we then look at political mediation and peace operations in parallel, we find the following dynamics.

Top-level or top-down approaches are more suitable to unlock legal authorization, political support and funds from the UN; and where players beyond the level of the RECs are involved or have strong interests. They are also required for demanding military operations that require intelligence and logistics. Bottom-level or bottom-up approaches are more suitable where lasting political solutions are sought, where rapid deployment in the vicinity of a capable troop-contributing country is required, and where the legitimacy of global actors is strongly contested.

The inherent contradictions between these two dynamics can severely hamper efforts in crisis management. But there is no 'one formula' that resolves these contradictions. Rather, the AU, the RECs and the UN should hone their skills to find practical solutions that take both dynamics into account. Subsidiarity cuts both ways.

Conclusion

The issue of subsidiarity has been at the heart of the discussion on the APSA for a number of years. The 2010 assessment of the APSA by the AU itself has put forward quite a number of pertinent observations and recommendations in this regard, prominent among them the need for a special MoU between the AU and the RECs/RMs with regard to peace operations (African Union 2010). There seems to be no easy solution. The issue of subsidiarity and the AU–REC relationship as a whole is too complex to be resolved quickly. The outcomes of the 2010 APSA assessment should warn us that a clear understanding of this relationship, transformed into mandates and processes, may not be in reach for the next couple of years. Arguably, this is not only a conceptual issue, but also requires various centres of power and influence to work together and find solutions that balance their respective interests and relative weight.

But the capability of the AU to mandate, mount and conduct peace operations should not be held hostage by this discussion. It would be wrong for Africa to tie the fate of its own peace operations capacity to this overall relationship issue. What is needed now is an effort to untie the knot of AU–REC/RM relationships in the area of peace operations and, through a reaffirmed vision of an African intervention capability, come to solutions that both reflect the principles set out in 2002 and 2004 and provide a pragmatic response to today's challenges.

Finally, the relevance of the principle of subsidiarity and its various interpretations in each prevailing circumstance should also be analysed within the context of a paradigm shift from state to regional security and to human security. It should be looked at in line with future scenarios of a horizontal relationship rather than a vertical one – how best to achieve new collaboration and harmonization models and the consolidation of the multidimensional concept of peace operations in the best interests of their effective deployment in Africa.

Notes

1 'Africa, through the African Union, plays a central role in bringing about peace, security and stability on the Continent' (Preamble of the PSC Protocol).

2 'Regional Mechanisms' in this clause is today generally understood as referring to the RECs.

3 One may ask whether the SADC commitment by its member states to contribute to AU peace operations only if and when the SADC itself agrees is congruent with the AU protocol.

4 The five permanent members of the UN Security Council.

5 Ethiopian invasion forces stayed throughout and were eventually folded into AMISOM in January 2014. Kenya invaded Somalia in October 2011, and its troops were folded into AMISOM in February 2012.

6 The AU PSC called for the establishment of MISMA, which became AFISMA only through a UNSC Resolution in December 2012.

7 Actually the MNJTF had already

been created in 1998 by Nigeria, Chad and Niger, to deal with crime in their border regions.

8 *Inter alia* by way of requesting a special US$1 billion as an external loan.

9 It should be noted that there was a discussion within the UNSC as to whether an ECOWAS mission could be backed without the consent of the AU PSC, but it appears that this idea was rejected.

References

African Union (2002) *Protocol Relating to the Establishment of the Peace and Security Council of the African Union*, Durban: African Union, www.peaceau.org/uploads/psc-protocol-en.pdf, accessed 18 November 2015.

— (2005) *Roadmap for the Operationalization of the African Standby Force*, AU document EXP/AU-RECs/ASF/4(1), Addis Ababa: African Union, http://www.operationspaix.net/DATA/DOCUMENT/5675~v~Roadmap_for_the_operationalization_of_the_African_Standby_Force.pdf, accessed 18 November 2015.

— (2008) *MOU AUC – RECS/RMs in Peace and Security*, Addis Ababa: African Union, www.peaceau.org/uploads/mou-au-rec-eng.pdf.

— (2010) *APSA Assessment Report*, Addis Ababa: African Union, www.securitycouncilreport.org/atf/cf/%7B65BFCF9B-6D27-4E9C-8CD3-CF6E4FF96FF9%7D/RO%20African%20Peace%20and%20Security%20Architecture.pdf, accessed 18 November 2015.

Ancas, S. (2011) 'The effectiveness of regional peacemaking in Southern Africa – problematising the United Nations–African Union–Southern African Development Community relationship', *African Journal on Conflict Resolution*, XI(1): 129–52.

De Coning, C., L. Gelot and J. Karlsrud (2015) *Strategic Options for the Future of African Peace Operations: 2015–2025*, Oslo/Uppsala: Norwegian Institute of International Affairs/Nordic Africa Institute.

Hutchful, E. (1999) 'The ECOMOG experience with peacekeeping in West Africa', in M. Malan (ed.), *Whither Peacekeeping in Africa?*, ISS Monograph no. 36, Pretoria: Institute of Security Studies (ISS).

Likoti, F. J. (2007) 'The 1998 military intervention in Lesotho: SADC peace mission or resource war?', *International Peacekeeping*, 14(2): 251–63.

Mays, T. (2009) *AMISOM – why did it successfully deploy after the failure of the IGASOM?*, United Nations Peace Support Operations Training Centre, cdn.peaceopstraining.org/theses/mays.pdf, accessed 18 November 2015.

Ngoma, N. (2004) 'Hawks, doves or penguins? A critical review of the SADC military intervention in the DRC', ISS Paper 88, pp. 1–16.

Théroux-Bénoni, L. A. (2013a) *Lessons from the Malian crisis for the international security architecture*, Pretoria: Institute for Security Studies, http://isnblog.ethz.ch/international-relations/lessons-from-the-malian-crisis-for-the-international-security-architecture, accessed 18 November 2015.

Usman-Janguza, M. (2014) 'Did the Nigerian army actually succeed in ending the Liberian and Sierra-Leonean civil wars?', Blog, 10 August, janguzaarewa.blogspot.se/2014/08/did-nigerian-army-actually-succeed-in.html, accessed 18 November 2015.

5 | The strategic relationship between the African Union and its partners

Linda Darkwa

Introduction

The interrelated nature of global security has fostered enhanced cooperation in international relations and led to the strengthening of collective security arrangements. In Africa, an interaction of factors, including the continent's socio-political history, geostrategic relevance and governance realities, influences its security landscape. The security challenges confronting Africa affect other regions of the world just as much as the threats of other continents affect Africa. Consequently, significant interest has been generated among various actors interested in enhancing peace and security on the continent as a way of guaranteeing peace and security in their specific parts of the world in particular and in the world at large.

To a large extent, this interest has been generated in part by the signalled determination of African leaders to proactively address security threats on the continent through the transformation of the continent's collective security mechanism, the Organization of African Unity (OAU), into the African Union (AU). The provision by the drafters of the Constitutive Act of a legal basis for intervening in the so-called domestic affairs of states and the establishment of an institutional framework to operationalize this provision offered the most concrete expression of the commitment of Africa's leaders to engage in a fundamentally new way on matters of peace and security.

Beyond the legal provisions and institutional establishment, the AU has, since coming into force in 2002, engaged in a profoundly new way in the search for peace on the continent. From its earlier engagements of overseeing the implementation of ceasefire arrangements, the AU has taken on significantly more challenging endeavours through its practice of robust and proactive deployments – seeking political engagement where no ceasefire agreements exist, as in Somalia, deploying into Darfur and responding in a timely manner to crisis situations in Mali and the Central African Republic (CAR) among others. In this new engagement, African Union member states have contributed the most fundamental resource – mission personnel – to all of its operations. This notwithstanding, the AU is confronted with capability challenges that hamper its efforts in a number of areas. This has encouraged the development of unique partnerships between itself and several stakeholders through multilateral and bilateral platforms.

External partners have contributed, through the provision of experts, finance, logistics and training, to African operations. Given the UN's extensive experience and capabilities in peace operations, it has offered considerable support to peace operations in Africa. In Somalia, the United Nations Support Office (UNSOA) to the African Union Mission to Somalia (AMISOM) has supported the AU mission with considerable logistics. The European Union (EU) has also provided financial support to almost all of the AU's peace operations – the African Union Mission in Sudan (AMIS), AMISOM, the African-led International Support Mission in Mali (AFISMA), the African Union Mission in the Central African Republic (known by its French acronym MISCA) as well as the African Union Regional Task Force for the Elimination of the LRA (LRA–RTF). In 2005, the North Atlantic Treaty Organization (NATO) provided support to the AU for the deployment of AMIS in the form of strategic lift, training and the use of intelligence (Reichard 2006: 56). Individual countries such as Norway, Sweden, Saudi Arabia, the United Kingdom, Japan and the United States of America, among others, have also contributed in various ways to peace operations in Africa. In most instances, partners have provided strategic lift and strategic communication capabilities, as well as remuneration for personnel. Although some of the assistance provided forms part of long-term existing frameworks of engagement, and is therefore predictable, some is negotiated on an ad hoc basis and is therefore unpredictable.

This chapter examines the strategic relationship between the AU and its partners in relation to the maintenance of peace and security on the continent. Using secondary and primary sources of information, it provides a trajectory of the AU's relationships in the area of peace and security and chronicles the issues that require reform. Subsequent to the introduction, the first section of the chapter discusses the concept of strategic partnerships generally, while the second discusses the AU and its strategic partnerships in particular. The third section discusses the capability needs of the AU and the fourth proffers options for strengthening the AU's strategic partnerships for future peace operations.

The concept of strategic partnerships

Although it has almost become a buzzword in multilateral discourses, the concept of strategic partnerships lacks a single definition. Cameron and Zheng (2007: 4) define it as 'a long-term commitment by two important actors to establish a close relationship across a significant number of policy areas. This does not mean that there will be no differences between the partners (after all, differences within a marriage are not unknown), but that the partners recognize the importance of their commitment to each other and are prepared to try and reach common ground wherever possible.' According to Giovanni Grevi

(2010: 1), strategic partnerships are relationships that are essential to the mutual attainment of the goals of the parties involved. The defining characteristic that distinguishes strategic partnerships from other forms of partnerships is the fact that while strategic partners are well positioned to mutually support one another, they also have the ability to inflict significant harm on one another (ibid.: 2). Put differently, strategic partners have the ability to help or hurt one another and, as a result, are essential to the realization of the goals of one another.

Strategic partnerships are predicated on the assumptions that the parties have some shared values and norms at least in the area of partnership; clear objectives and goals (Grevi 2010; Cameron and Zheng 2007: 7); the ability to clearly articulate their interests and needs in the context of the partnership; and capabilities to help one another realize their objectives and goals. The most essential elements that underpin any strategic partnership are (i) a shared need and (ii) the ability to deliver (Cameron and Zheng 2007: 2). Although the need may not necessarily be immediate or even related directly to the situation at hand, it must be something that all partners perceive to be necessary for their well-being. It is general knowledge that a present situation could have repercussions either in the short, medium or long term on the interests of cooperating partners. Strategic partnerships must therefore have a long-term outlook and be sufficiently comprehensive and holistic (ibid.: 8). There must also be constant interaction between strategic partners since there can be no relationship when the interaction between the entities is only occasional or on an ad hoc basis. Cameron and Zheng (ibid.: 8) stress that a strategic partnership must have 'an intensive, on-going and stable commitment to it'.

Ideally, a strategic partnership is between two equal entities. However, this need not always be a precondition as the defining characteristic of any such partnership must be a shared need. In security cooperation, strategic relationships may be formed between unequal entities if they are confronted with a common threat that requires a concerted effort to address and defeat it. As a result, unlike in other areas of strategic partnerships, strategic partnerships in the areas of peace and security may be between two or more states, between states and multilateral institutions and between two or more multilateral institutions. Although this means that there may be unequal entities entering into strategic partnerships, this need not create major challenges since despite the socio-political and financial differences, each partner comes to the table with identifiable strengths that are indispensable to meeting the shared need either in the immediate or mid to long term.

The AU and its strategic partnerships

The objectives of the AU may be summarized broadly as the promotion of continental unity, socio-economic development, peace and security, and the promotion and protection of the interests of Africa in the international community (African Union 2000: Article 3). Aware of the fact that none of the objectives set out in the Act could be realized without peace and security, the founders of the Union made a proviso in the preamble of the Constitutive Act to the effect that 'the scourge of conflicts in Africa constitutes a major impediment to the socio-economic development of the continent and of the need to promote peace, security and stability as a prerequisite for the implementation of our development and integration agenda'. The primary need of the Union is therefore the maintenance of peace and security on the continent. This need must therefore be the standard against which every strategic partnership of the Union is benchmarked.

Generally, the Union's existing partnerships are cast in four main forms and include the traditional continent–continent partnerships; the multilateral institution to multilateral institution partnerships; the continent to country partnerships; and the continent to region partnerships. Despite the Union's numerous partnerships, only two are generally referred to in the public narratives as strategic; these are the partnerships with the European Union and the United Nations. These two partnerships are well structured, with defined mechanisms for constant interactions.

The AU and its strategic partnerships in the context of peace operations As already indicated, strategic partnerships are formed on the basis of shared values, goals and interests. As a collective security organization, the AU is undergirded by two fundamental values and norms – sovereignty as responsibility and non-indifference. Thus, although the Constitutive Act acknowledges the twin principles of sovereignty and non-interference, it also arrogates to itself the right of intervention in certain defined circumstances – in the event of war crimes, genocide and crimes against humanity.[1] It is the only international organization that provides a legal basis for the normative principle of the 'Responsibility to Protect'.

Articles 4(e), (h) and (j) of the Constitutive Act provide the legal principles for addressing issues of peace and security on the continent. Article 4(e) provides for the pacific settlement of conflicts with assistance from the Union, while Articles 4(h) and (j) provide the legal justification for peace enforcement and an opportunity for member states to request assistance from the Union for the restoration of peace and security respectively. These two provisions have a more expanded scope on the exceptions to the use of force than the traditional caveats provided for under international law. First, Article 4(h) allows the Union to intervene as a party to the conflict, thereby ignoring the classical principles of consent, neutrality and impartiality that underpin traditional peacekeeping operations. Secondly, Article 4(j) allows member states to request assistance from the Union 'in order to restore peace and security'.

To give meaning to its norms of responsible sovereignty and non-indifference in the face of war crimes, genocide and crimes against humanity, the AU's APSA has clearly delineated institutions for the prevention, management and resolution of conflicts. Although the AU's most well-known peacemaking efforts are its security interventions, it is engaged in the full gamut of peacemaking and has utilized its special envoys and the Panel of the Wise to undertake several preventive and peacemaking missions on the continent. While some of these missions have succeeded in averting the escalation of conflicts into violence, others have been less successful. In a few instances, the Union has made some avoidable mistakes by not adhering to the principles of preventive diplomacy and peacemaking. It has been noted that although the structures for peacemaking provided by the Union have the potential of addressing several of the conflicts on the continent, there is the need to provide the right tools and skills for those deployed in non-military peacemaking on the continent.

Under the auspices of Article 4(j), the AU has been engaged in different forms of peacekeeping missions on the continent. In Burundi (2003) and Sudan (2004), the Union's interventions were based on existing ceasefire agreements, while the deployment in the Comoros in 2006 was at the invitation of the parties to the conflict. The rest of the Union's interventions have taken place in non-benign environments. For example, the mandate of the AU's Mission in Somalia (AMISOM) requires the mission to 'take all necessary measures, as appropriate, and in coordination with the Somalia National Defence and Public Safety Institutions, to reduce the threat posed by al-Shabaab and other armed opposition groups' (African Union 2014). In 2012, the deployment of the African-led International Support Mission to Mali (AFISMA) was in response to a request by Mali for assistance to protect its territorial integrity and recover the northern parts of its territory that had been occupied by terrorist groups. In another development, the deployment in 2013 of the African-led International Support Mission to the CAR (MISCA) was authorized by the AU Peace and Security Council (PSC) for the protection of civilians, stabilization and assistance for security sector reform among other objectives. In almost all of the above instances (with the exception of Comoros), the UN took over the missions after the attainment of a degree of security and stability by the AU.

The AU's peacekeeping doctrine is reflective of the changed contemporary security landscape. Confronted with intra-state armed conflicts that are often waged by faceless combatants, it has become increasingly difficult to engage in political processes of peacemaking. The practice of the AU has therefore shifted to create conditions that make it possible to undertake the political process of peacemaking. Deviating from the traditional principles of peacekeeping, the AU, with the blessing of the UN, has deployed troops for battle in a number of instances, including in Somalia, Mali and the CAR.

As a regional organization acting under Chapter VIII of the Charter, the AU's ability to undertake enforcement and war-fighting missions is subject to the authorization of the UNSC. That the UNSC has given its approval and authorization for such missions in different circumstances is an indication of its acknowledgement that the changed security threats confronting the world require a paradigm shift from the traditional notion of peacekeeping to a much more robust posture. Yet, given the divergent stances of the veto-wielding members of the Council, a doctrinal shift from the traditional principles of peacekeeping by the UN is highly unlikely in the near future. It is therefore convenient for the UN to operate through the legal and practical arrangements of the AU that allow it to enforce peace when there is no peace to keep. While this doctrinal shift by the AU provides tools for effectively addressing the dire security challenges confronting the continent, it means that its strategic partners must share the norms undergirding the doctrine and be supportive of the practice adopted to ensure that the partnerships deliver.

The capability needs in AU peace operations

Today's security challenges, which are generated and sustained by the exploitation of grievances, relative deprivation, exclusion, marginalization and religious fundamentalism and extremism, among other factors, are also often conducted in urban spaces, with little or no attention to the principles of humanity, distinction, proportionality and military necessity that have traditionally guided the conduct of armed conflict. The challenge of addressing these conflicts has been compounded in several instances by the anonymity of the actors driving the insecurity agenda, which makes it difficult to utilize non-violent mechanisms of conflict resolution to prevent and/or manage such conflicts. These dynamics create peculiar challenges for peace operations and make it imperative for deployed missions to possess certain capabilities.

Notwithstanding the demonstrated commitment of the AU to addressing the security challenges of the continent, there are a myriad of challenges that militate against its successes. Since strategic partnerships are values-oriented and needs-based, it is important for the needs in peace operations in Africa to be reflected in the considerations that guide the formation of the AU's strategic partnerships.

The need to appreciate the changed nature of security and the emerging doctrine of peace enforcement The new security challenges confronting the world have significant implications for peace operations. The evidence of twenty-first-century peace operations indicates that the traditional notion of peacekeeping, which was predicated on existing ceasefire agreements, is increasingly becoming a thing of the past. Instead, peace operations personnel are being deployed into active conflict situations with high volatility, where peacekeepers have to fight extremist and fundamentalist groups. However, notwithstanding the changes in the global security landscape, there has been little change in the global security architecture, as the UN has not been able to adapt its processes to be able to meet the security challenges confronting the world. The UN therefore piggybacks on the AU's pragmatic posture of creating peace by authorizing peace enforcement missions that are essentially war-fighting missions, and taking over only when there is peace to be kept. This arrangement serves the AU and its partners quite well because, through its doctrinal shift, the AU is undertaking activities that help to minimize the threats to international peace and security from the African continent, which would otherwise have been the responsibility of the UNSC. Through its efforts to mitigate the threats posed to international peace and security, the AU's efforts also help to address some of the threats posed to other regional actors with close proximity to the continent.

However, although the AU and its RECs/RMs have become the first responders to these security challenges, their missions are heavily under-resourced and under-equipped. Although the popular press suggests that the larger the threat confronted the larger the resources, the AU's missions are working contrari-wise. So while the African peace operations have wider mandates in complex contexts, they have limited resources in terms of troops, requisite equipment and other logistics. Despite several recommendations, including those contained in the Prodi report on the cooperation of the United Nations and regional organizations to make UN-accessed funding available in the short term for UN-authorized African peace operations, this has not as yet materialized.

Current funding arrangements, which include the use of pledged resources, have resulted in a number of complexities as these funds are often unpredictable and their availability mired in conditionalities that are incompatible with the character of contemporary peace operations. For instance, the foreign policies of some contributing states that prohibit the use of funds to procure lethal equipment for peace operations clearly demonstrate a lack of appreciation of the contexts within which peace operations in Africa are being deployed, since it is impractical to expect missions engaged in fighting and in need of lethal equipment not to use available resources to meet their needs.

It is unfortunate that the AU is unable to provide a substantial amount of the financial and logistical resources needed for the peace operations on the continent. However, it is important to acknowledge that while the AU and its member states have not to date provided substantial financial resources, they have provided the boots on the ground that are so critical to the new types of peace operations being mandated. Since the AU's doctrinal shift is to the benefit of the international community, it is essential for the international community to share the burden of such missions. Currently, the EU shoulders a substantial part of the budget of AMISOM. Without this assistance, it would have been near impossible to sustain AMISOM's activities in Somalia.

The need for effective engagement in efficient capacity development As Aning &
Abdallah (Chapter 2) have shown earlier in this book, the African continent
is confronted by overwhelming security threats. The increasing use of terrorist
strategies in armed conflict situations, the rise in religious extremism and
fundamentalism and the interplay between transnational organized crime and
terrorism in armed conflict situations requires that personnel being deployed
in the theatre of operations have the requisite training and assets. Given the
novelty of some of these threats and the fact that training in security institutions is often based on national needs, there are training gaps that must be
addressed to develop the capacity of those being deployed on missions.

On the other hand, there is an underutilization of capacity that is partly
due to the lack of coordination between the AU and its partners. Although
a number of bilateral initiatives for peace operation training exist between
African states and external partners, training has not matched deployment, as
many of those trained do not get deployed. This is attributable to a number
of reasons, which include the lack of coordination between partners and the
AU on their capacity development initiatives on the continent. It must be
stated that although there is no need for all bilateral initiatives to be brought
to the attention of the AU, it is prudent for the AU to be informed of peace
operation capacity development since the capacities are most likely to be
utilized by the AU. Such coordination could provide opportunities to identify
the current peace operation training needs on the continent.

There are also deficits in capacity development of preventive action based
on the AU's identified capacity needs. The AU is the sum total of its member
states, which operate mainly through the various RECs/RMs. It is therefore
important to ensure that the capacities of the RECs/RMs are also developed
to enable them to play meaningful complementary roles in guaranteeing
peace and security on the continent. Although some of the ongoing capacity
development initiatives provided by the UN and other partners are relevant,
a number of them do not necessarily meet the capacity development needs
of the Union. The AU has itself undergone significant transformation in the
area of capacity development and can now boast of a significant number of
experts and specialists with adequate knowledge in a number of areas. There
is therefore a need for partners to acknowledge the capacity available at the
Commission and the RECs/RMs in order to be able to work with them on
areas of priority to ensure that the development of needed capacity enhances
the effectiveness and efficiency of peace operations in Africa.

*The need for a common understanding of and approach to peace opera-
tions* There is undoubtedly an improved relationship between the AU and its
partners in the area of cooperation for peace operations. This notwithstanding,
there are a number of tenuous areas that need better clarity. These include

the lack of a common understanding and appreciation of conflict dynamics, which in turn leads to the lack of a common approach to addressing the issues involved in conflicts. This has led to divergent views on the policies, processes and actions needed to address such conflicts and has in some instances contributed to delays in taking needed actions. This challenge has been exacerbated by the interference of former colonial powers with particular interests in the affected states and has often led to multiple uncoordinated interventions during peace operations.

Strategic partnerships for AU peace operations – the way forward

The relationship between the AU and its strategic partners has not been without challenges. Delays in the release and disbursement of funds and the lack of predictable funding are among the main challenges the AU has faced, and continues to face. The Union's partners, on the other hand, appear to be frustrated with its failure to clearly articulate its strategic needs in a timely manner. In some instances, in line with their funding regulations, partners have had to withdraw pledged funding because of the Union's inability to spend committed resources. It is important to acknowledge the fact that a safe and stable Africa would be to the benefit of all stakeholders as it would be a step towards the attainment of the UN's own objective of guaranteeing international peace and security. As a result, working together to achieve the envisaged end-state should be a priority for the international community as a whole.

The need for enhanced cooperation between the AU and its partners Even though the cooperation between the AU and its partners has improved considerably, there is still ample room for improvement. To be able to harness the comparative advantage of each of the partners interested in peace operations in Africa, it is imperative to have a common approach to addressing the security challenges from the very beginning. This means that there must be a common understanding and appreciation of the issues at stake, the identification of capabilities required to address the challenges and of the partners that have comparative advantage in that regard. This would allow for the identification of a lead organization based on comparative advantage and the assignment of complementary roles to enhance the effectiveness of the engagement, which in turn would minimize the competition that has characterized a number of peace operations and guarantee that available capabilities are harnessed to enhance the efficiency of peace operations.

Comprehensive strategic needs to guide the partnerships As a first step, the needs of peace operations on the continent must be better articulated. Through joint comprehensive analysis, the needs of peace operations in Africa must be identified so that they can be addressed in a systematic manner by all stakeholders. There are several commissioned reports that detail the needs of peace operations on the continent. A synthesis of these reports could shine light on what is needed, what has been provided and what is outstanding in peace operations on the continent.

A cohesive approach to preventive action The nature and scope of the current security threats confronting the continent are significantly different from the threats of the immediate post-Cold War era. Constitutional *coup d'états*, piracy, terrorism and other forms of transnational crime appear to be the contemporary security threats confronting the continent. Although these threats have the propensity to affect the peace and stability of the continent, they do not fall within the context of Articles 4(h) and 4(j). The AU may therefore be constrained in its ability to effectively address such issues through the use of force. There is therefore a need for the AU and its partners to pay more attention to the structures for peacemaking provided for in the pillars of the APSA.

Predictable and effective means of funding The AU and its partners need to establish clearer systems of funding. There is the unfinished debate at the UN on whether funds for African peace operations should come from accessed funds or the trust fund. The AU's experience with trust funds has shown that it is not the best option in the current peace operation landscape as pledges are not always easy to redeem. Going forward, this is an area where the influence of the Union's strategic partners may be needed to leverage the nay-sayers who have been against the use of accessed funds for start-up missions. However, the AU must also have an honest discussion with its member states and regions on ways of raising alternative sources of funding for peace operations on the continent.

Conclusion

The fact that the report of the UN secretary general's High-level Independent Panel on Peace Operations singled out strategic partnerships with African institutions affirms the substantial role being played by the AU and the RECs/RMs in the maintenance of regional and international peace and security. Its prescriptions for a mutually beneficial relationship provide guidelines for the development of various types of strategic partnerships on the continent. While the recommendation for a UN assessed contribution is undoubtedly limited to the UN, the report's call for 'consultative decision making and common strategy; division of labour based on respective comparative advantage; joint analysis, planning, monitoring and evaluation; integrated response to the conflict cycle, including prevention and transparency, accountability and respect for international standards' provides signposts for present and future strategic partnerships on the continent.

Since the primary objective of the Union as articulated in various documents is the maintenance of peace and security, which are considered prerequisites for the socio-economic development of the continent, it is imperative for its peace operation needs to be reflected in its strategic partnerships. In this regard, two models of strategic partnerships may be considered – one that reflects the continent's security and peace operation needs generally as a backdrop and a more specific one that is solely focused on the continent's security and peace operation needs. As a final word, it is important to ensure that the decision made reflects the practice of the peace operations of the past and envisages the needs of the future.

Note

1 Article 4(h) of the Constitutive Act arrogates to the Union the right to 'intervene in a Member State pursuant to a decision of the Assembly in respect of grave circumstances, namely war crimes, genocide and crimes against humanity'.

References

African Union (2000) *The Constitutive Act of the African Union*, Lome: African Union, http://www.au.int/en/sites/default/files/ConstitutiveAct_EN.pdf, accessed 18 November 2015.

— (2014) *AMISOM Mandate*, Addis Ababa: African Union, amisom-au.org/amisom-mandate/, accessed 1 December 2014.

Cameron, F. and Y. Zheng (2007) 'Key elements of a strategic partnership', in S. Crossick and E. Reuter (eds), *China–EU: A Common Future*, London: World Scientific Publications.

Grevi, G. (2010) *Making EU strategic partnerships effective*, Madrid: FRIDE, fride.org/download/WP105_Making_EU_Strategic_ENG_dic10.pdf, accessed 18 November 2015.

Reichard, M. (2006) *The EU–NATO Relationship: A Legal and Political Perspective*, Aldershot: Ashgate, cited in P. Pryce, 'Toward a NATO–African Union partnership: structuring future engagement', *Baltic Security and Defence Review*, XIV(2), 2012:56.

6 | Mission support for African peace operations

Walter Lotze

Introduction

Over the last ten years, the AU and the RECs and RMs have become major actors in relation to the deployment of peace operations. Accordingly, significant effort has gone into the training of personnel and enhancing the capabilities of African troop- and police-contributing countries, and into developing the planning and mandating capacities of the AU and the regional organizations and mechanisms which enable them to deploy peace operations. However, the development of effective and efficient mission support systems, which underpin the workings of a peace operation once deployed, has been heavily neglected to date. Indeed, the development of mission support concepts, frameworks, systems and procedures is likely the biggest gap in the development of the ASF to date. Unfortunately, this is also a major stumbling block in terms of current and future African peace operations, as effective and efficient support systems are a critical enabler, or turnkey, for any peace operation, without which the conduct of operations becomes all but impossible.

As a result of the gaps which have arisen in this area, four broad models of mission support (lead nation model, bilateral support model, trust fund model and support package model), which are heavily reliant on the role of partners, have developed over the course of the past decade in response to the growing operational requirements. While these models have enabled the conduct of the operations which have been deployed to date, they all have inherent shortcomings, and have prevented the AU and the RECs/RMs from being able to independently deploy and sustain peace operations. In effect, therefore, the mission support models which have been developed to date have made African actors entirely reliant on partner support for the deployment and sustainment of African peace operations. If the ASF is to reach full operational capability, and if African states wish to play a greater role in relation to peace and security on the continent, this gap needs to be urgently addressed.

This chapter traces the developments which have taken place to date at a conceptual and policy level in relation to mission support for the ASF and African peace operations, before identifying the four broad models of mission support which have arisen over the course of the past decade, and the implications which these pose for current and future operations. The financing mechanisms of these operations, and of the support models which have been developed, will also be briefly explored. Finally, the chapter will look at how these challenges, which must be tackled if the ASF is to reach full operational capability and African peace operations are to be strengthened going forward, can be addressed.

Mission support models for African peace operations

The ASF policy framework, adopted in 2003, provided the initial framework for the conceptual development of mission support frameworks for African peace operations. In light of the rapid deployment timelines which were envisaged for most ASF operations (fourteen days for an urgent intervention, thirty days for smaller observer missions, and ninety days for larger operations), the policy framework recommended that the AU should develop an appropriate concept for a mission support system that was largely reliant on a Continental Logistics Base (CLB) and a system of Regional Logistics Bases (RLBs), as well as the support services which member states, in their roles as troop-contributing countries (TCCs), could provide. As such, the AU Commission was placed largely in a policy development and coordination role, and entrusted with the establishment and operations of the logistics base at the continental level, while the regions were tasked with the direct management of regional logistics infrastructures, including the Regional Logistics Bases, with TCCs carrying the bulk of the in-theatre mission support requirements, possibly through frameworks established by lead nations. Further, the policy framework recommended that, as AU operations were likely to transition into United Nations (UN) operations relatively quickly, the AU and the UN should establish cooperation frameworks in the area of mission support (African Union 2003: 3–25).

On the issue of funding ASF operations, the policy framework recommended that African states give consideration to additional means of generating funds, including the establishment of a peace tax at the level of the regions, or the use of assessed contributions at the level of the AU to cover the operating costs of peace operations. To handle this volume of funding, the policy framework further recommended that the necessary financial systems and procedures be established at the level of the AU Commission (ibid.: 33).

Since the adoption of the policy framework, little in the way of additional guidance has been developed. A draft mission support concept was developed prior to 2009, which did provide a definition of mission support as 'a broad concept embracing all those elements required to support the mission including administration and logistics'. According to this definition, mission support in the ASF context includes (a) the design and development, acquisition, storage, movement, distribution, maintenance, modification, evacuation, disposition and disposal of materiel, (b) transportation, including strategic lift, (c) personnel and legal issues, (d) acquisition or construction, maintenance, operation and disposition of facilities, (e) acquisition or furnishing of services, and (f) health support services (African Union n.d. b: 2). The concept relies heavily on military logistics provided by TCCs, or on the provision of common services by the RECs/RMs, with the AU Commission playing a guidance, oversight and reimbursement role. A heavy emphasis is also placed on self-sustainment by the military forces in a deployment, with a minor role foreseen for civilian contractors, and only in the role of force augmentation, and not to replace capability in force planning (ibid.: 13).

A concept of mission support for the ASF RDC was also developed in 2009, with a focus on enabling the AU to rapidly engage a force of about 2,500 personnel to respond to an emergency situation within a period of fourteen days following a mandate. The concept differs significantly from the ASF mission support concept above, as it relies heavily on the AU providing strategic airlift for the RDC, as well as providing tactical aviation assets and support and engineering assets. This central provision of key support functions is, then, as per the concept, to be complemented by voluntary contributions of strategic lift and other support functions by member states, even if these are not a part of the RDC deployment (African Union n.d. a: 1–6).

In 2008, the East African Standby Force (EASF) developed a more comprehensive approach to mission support, and produced a support manual for operations undertaken under the ASF. This in turn was further developed by the AU Peace Support Operations Division (AU PSOD) and released in draft format again in 2014. The conceptual approach to mission support was still defined as 'a broad concept embracing all those elements required to support the mission including administration and logistics' (African Union 2014: 10–11). The approach developed here, however, divides the support functions into two broad categories, namely integrated support services and administrative services, but places most emphasis on the logistics function within the integrated support services. Notably, functions such as procurement, supply, facility management, movement control, transport, engineering, medical services, budget and administration are all placed under the logistics function in this approach. Another significant change in the approach to mission support relates to the self-sustainment period of TCCs, which is reduced to fifteen days, after which the regions are expected to provide fifteen days of sustainment. After this initial thirty-day period, the AU is then expected to take over responsibility for the provision of all support services on the basis of contractual arrangements with civilian contractors (ibid.: 16–17).

In addition, the roles and responsibilities divided between the AU Commission, the planning elements at the level of the regions and the contributing countries differ significantly from those originally conceived of in the ASF policy framework. The AU Commission is tasked with budgeting and securing funds for mission expenses, contracting service providers and providing all centralized support services within thirty days of deployment, providing strategic lift on the basis of commercial contracting or letters of assist with TCCs, establishing the necessary infrastructure in the mission area, and managing all support services and administration in the mission area. The regions in turn are tasked with providing guidance to the TCCs and PCCs to ensure standardization, providing support through the Regional Logistics Bases where required, providing mounting bases for operations, and providing fifteen days of support as a bridging mechanism between contributing country self-sustainment and the initiation of centralized support services by the AU. Contributing countries (TCCs/PCCs) are tasked with preparing their personnel and providing the necessary equipment for their deployment, movement from their countries of origin to mounting bases, and with providing the initial fifteen days of self-sustainment until regional support for the next fifteen days of sustainment is initiated (ibid.: 17–18).

It is clear, therefore, that several concepts of mission support have been developed to date, none of which is much aligned to the others. Importantly, each of these concepts assigns different roles and responsibilities to the AU Commission, the regional planning elements and the contributing countries, providing for a range of engagement that is quite broad. It should also be noted that beyond the ASF policy framework, the mission support concepts which have been developed are all in draft format, and no further approved document on mission support for the ASF or current peace operations exists in the AU context. There is as such no agreed mission support framework which informs the planning, deployment and management of contemporary African peace operations.

In addition to this gap at the policy level, the implementation of the mission support concept which was developed in the ASF policy framework has also been slow to date. The notion of establishing logistics bases at continental and regional levels has not developed much beyond the conceptual stages. In 2011, a site for the CLB was identified in Douala, Cameroon, and significant effort went into conducting feasibility assessments and developing the initial site plans for the facility. Since 2012, however, no further progress has been made in this regard. The development of Regional Logistics Bases (RLBs) is even farther behind, with some regions having identified potential sites, and others moving away from the concept of maintaining a regional facility altogether. The investments made in developing mission support expertise and management capacities at the planning elements have also been uneven to date, with varying levels of capacity at the AU PSOD and the regional planning elements in place. The initial notion of building on the military logistics capacities which TCCs bring into an operation to develop support systems for the entire mission has also largely not held up consistently, mainly for two reasons. First, experience has shown that contributing countries have uneven capabilities in the area of logistics and other support functions, and not all TCCs are able to deploy the required capabilities to meet mission support requirements for a peace support operation. Secondly, while some TCCs are able to meet the initial fifteen- or thirty-day self-sustainment requirements, others are not, and are thus dependent on a full range of support services on arrival in an operational area, which the AU, the regions and other TCCs are not able to meet.

As a result of these gaps at the policy and operational levels, the AU and the RECs/RMs have in effect since the commencement of the ASF project not developed functioning support models which can effectively deploy and sustain peace operations when required, and the operations which have been deployed over the course of the past decade have been deployed in the absence of any functioning mission support framework. As a result, ad hoc support models have been developed in response to specific deployment requirements every time an African peace support operation has been mandated.

Papering over the gaps – four evolving mission support models

In response to a range of evolving deployment requirements, four general models of mission support have been developed for African peace operations, namely (1) the lead nation model, (2) the bilateral support model, (3) the trust fund model and (4) the support package model. Each of these will be explained briefly in further detail below, before the lessons which have been learned through the use of these models are reflected on.

1) Lead nation model Under the lead nation model, a lead nation serves as the framework country for the operation, providing the bulk of the strategic lift, the mission support requirements and the financing of the operation, either on the basis of a voluntary contribution, or on a cost-sharing, common cost or reimbursable basis, depending on the specific nature of the arrangements entered into between the lead nation and the mandating organization. This model was used in the case of the Economic Community of West African States (ECOWAS) deployments in Liberia and Sierra Leone in the 1990s and early 2000s, when Nigeria served as the lead nation. This was also the model used by the AU in the case of the African Union Mission in Burundi (AMIB) between 2003 and 2004, when South Africa played the role of a lead nation, providing the framework which enabled Ethiopia and Mozambique to deploy to the operation.

2) Bilateral support model Under the bilateral support model, bilateral partners, on a voluntary basis, provide support either to specific TCC or PCC operations within a mandated peace support operation directly, or provide support to a specific area of operations of the mission as a whole, through contracting and paying for the services of specialized service providers. This model has been used quite widely by partners, including by the United States, the United Kingdom, Canada, Germany, France and others, to support AU-mandated deployments in Darfur, Somalia, Mali and the CAR. Accordingly, specialist service providers – for instance, Pacific Architects and Engineers (PAE), Dyncorp, Bancroft, Mechem and others – have been contracted to provide services as diverse as camp construction and maintenance, catering, fuel, air operations and other services as required, with the bilateral partners directly covering these costs.

3) *Trust fund model* Under the trust fund model, the AU and/or the UN establish a trust fund, whereby member states can make voluntary financial contributions. The organization managing the trust fund then activates its procurement systems and uses these funds to contract specialist service providers to provide specific support to the operation, either as earmarked by the member state which has made the financial contribution, or to cover gaps in the support services which are not addressed by other means. This model has been used in the case of Somalia (UN-administered trust fund), Mali (AU-administered and UN-administered trust fund) and the CAR (UN-administered trust fund).

4) *Support package model* Finally, under the support package model, UN assessed contributions are utilized to establish and deliver a comprehensive support package for an African-mandated peace operation, similar in nature and scope to the support package that would be developed for a UN peacekeeping operation. Under this model, the entire mission support package is planned, managed and paid for by the UN, with the delivery of services the responsibility of service providers. This model has been used in Somalia, where the United Nations Support Office for AMISOM (UNSOA) was established in 2009, and administers a comprehensive support package for the African Union Mission in Somalia (AMISOM) of an annual value of approximately US$450 million, which is drawn from UN assessed contributions.

Each of the four support models referred to above has developed over time, in response to evolving crises, the dominant political and operational realities which have informed the responses to these specific crises, and the needs of the deploying organizations and the capabilities of the specific TCCs and PCCs. As has also been noted, in some operations several models have been used simultaneously. For instance, in the case of the AMISOM deployment in Somalia, the trust fund model, the bilateral support model and the support package model are all being used. In the case of the African-led International Support Mission to Mali (AFISMA) and the African-led International Support

Mission to the CAR (MISCA) deployments, both the bilateral support model and the trust fund model were used.

As such, these models have several strengths, when used in isolation or in combination with one another, as they have generally proved both flexible and able to respond to context-specific requirements, and on average the use of these models has allowed for support systems to be established relatively quickly when needed. Further, the models which were developed were based on the resources which were available at the time, and not on the basis of planning assumptions which could not be delivered later on. In addition, these models have allowed for the establishment of unique partnerships that leverage the strengths of the respective partners (AU–partners, AU–UN) to support the rapid deployment, and then the sustainment, of African peace operations to the field.

However, it is also equally clear that these models entail several inherent shortcomings. For one, the lack of predictability which they bring with them makes it extremely challenging for the AU and the RECs/RMs to plan for operations, as planners are not aware of which support model will be used and which resources will be available for the operation. When planning the deployment of AFISMA and MISCA, for instance, planners assumed that a UN support package, similar in nature to that being provided to AMISOM, would be put in place. Despite the AU having requested such a support package for AFISMA and MISCA, in both cases this was rejected by the UN Security Council. As such, support had to be patched together from those partners that were able to make contributions at the time, until the missions could be transitioned into UN peacekeeping operations.

For another, these models entail that the AU or the RECs/RMs do not have full control over their operations. Everything from fuel to rations to aviation assets and internet connectivity depends either on a TCC, or a bilateral partner, or the UN, or a combination of these. In the case of trust funds, the AU has not always had much say over the use of the funds which are pledged for its operations, with the trust funds administered by the UN. In the case of Mali in particular, the AU had very little insight into the trust fund for AFISMA and the use of the resources therein, leading to significant tensions between the AU and the UN in the transition of AFISMA into the United Nations Multidimensional Integrated Stabilization Mission in Mali (MINUSMA). As such, the AU's and the RECs/RMs' ability to effectively manage the operations they mandate is severely curtailed.

In addition, resource discrepancies and different standards have come to characterize African peace operations. Some operations receive higher levels of support than others, making it impossible for the AU to set and implement standards, and standardized systems, for its operations. It has also become clear that the level and standards of support for AU operations are lower than they are for equivalent UN operations, even where the UN is, through a trust fund or a logistical support package, providing support to an AU operation. This has led to considerable tensions over the implementation of the UNSOA mandate, for instance, where different standards are used by UNSOA to support UN operations in Somalia to those used for the AU operations in the same country. These discrepancies have also led to challenges in force generation. In the case of Mali, for instance, some countries were not willing to make pledged capabilities available for AFISMA, as they were waiting for the operation to transition into a UN peacekeeping mission in anticipation of receiving higher compensation and better support for their personnel. Another example was Darfur, where the transition from the African Union Mission in Sudan (AMIS) to the United Nations–African Union Mission in Darfur (UNAMID) witnessed a fourfold increase in the mission's support budget (Gelot et al. 2012: 12).

Further, it should be noted that transitions from AU to UN operations are made more challenging by support models which are less structured and predictable. In Mali, little investment was made in building up the capacity and the systems and procedures of AFISMA prior to the transition into MINUSMA, which impacted on MINUSMA's operations even two years after the transition. In the case of the CAR, however, more was invested, and the UN-administered trust fund used, to build up the capacities of the operation and its support systems prior to the transition, resulting in a much smoother transition from MISCA to MINUSCA.

A further shortcoming which is inherent to all the support models which have been developed to date is that none of these fully capture or respond to the requirements of dynamic high-intensity operations or the types of stabilization operations which the AU and the RECs/RMs have been undertaking, and are quite likely to undertake again in the future. In AMISOM, as shown clearly by Dersso (Chapter 3) in this volume, the consequences of such shortcomings are many. It is known that one armoured vehicle (Caspir) can lose more tyres in a month than an entire UN operation plans for in a year. By way of another example, in Somalia troops in some locations had to go for more than a year without proper water provision or purification, as the UN was not able to expand its operations at the same pace as the AMISOM operations were unfolding.

Overall, therefore, although various models of mission support have evolved which have enabled the AU and the RECs/RMs to deploy and sustain operations in the field, this has resulted in the creation of huge gaps in the development of effective and efficient mission support concepts, frameworks, systems and procedures for the ASF, as the AU and the RECs/RMs have not had to take responsibility for this area of their operations. Instead, each model of support is developed in an ad hoc manner, and largely left for missions to manage in the field. Accordingly, to date, no structured discussions on mission support concepts and frameworks have taken place between the AU and the RECs/RMs or the member states, and the AU and the RECs/RMs have not invested sufficiently in their own ability to plan for, and provide, mission support services across a range of possible deployment scenarios. In addition, and as discussed by Darkwa (Chapter 5) in this volume, the AU and the RECs/RMs have also not established a strategic relationship on the planning and management of support packages and services with the UN, the EU or bilateral partners which is forward-looking and provides an agreed framework on the parameters and modalities of cooperation.

Financing peace operations

An area in which some significant developments have taken place over the course of the past decade is in relation to funding mechanisms. The AU did establish a Peace Fund as envisioned by the *Protocol Relating to the Establishment of the Peace and Security Council of the African Union* (PSC Protocol), designed to provide the necessary financial resources for peace operations and other operational activities related to peace and security. The Peace Fund was intended to be resourced with financial contributions drawn from a percentage of the assessed contributions of member states, voluntary contributions from member states and other sources from within the African continent, as well as from partners (African Union 2002: Article 21). In addition, the PSC Protocol made provision for the utilization of assessed funding from member states, based on the scale of the contributions to the AU's regular budget, to cover the costs of a peace operation. However, the decision to use such assessed contributions needed to be taken by the appropriate policy organs of the AU on a case-by-case basis (ibid.). Despite the establishment of these mechanisms, however, to date the contributions made by member states to the Peace Fund have been somewhat erratic, as assessed contributions have been tied to the payment of membership dues by member states, which are often late or left unpaid. In addition, voluntary contributions to the Peace Fund by member states appear to have been few and far between. As such, the Peace Fund has not been a reliable source of funding, especially at the volume required to deploy and sustain peace operations. Further, the mechanism of assessed contributions was not activated to fund operations. Thus, while mechanisms have been established to fund operations, these have not yet been able to deliver the volume of funding required to cover the costs of the operations which have been deployed.

To address this gap, the European Union (EU) African Peace Facility (APF) was established in 2004, and has been the single most important financial mechanism underpinning African peace operations to date. By the end of 2013, the APF had contributed more than €1.2 billion to African peace operations and peace and security initiatives more broadly. Of the ongoing operations at the time, €575 million had been committed to AMISOM, €50 million to MISCA, and €2 million to the LRA–RTF. A further €443.7 million had been provided to the completed missions of AMIS, the AU's Operations in the Comoros (MAES), AFISMA and the Economic Community of Central African States (ECCAS) Mission for the Consolidation of Peace in the CAR (MICOPAX). In addition, the APF funds capacity development programmes and initiatives for the ASF, and through its Early Response Mechanism (ERM) supports conflict prevention, initial mediation activities, fact-finding missions and the planning phase for the deployment of new operations. On this basis alone, the ERM financed seven initiatives in the Sahel region, Sudan and South Sudan, the DRC, Mali, the CAR and Somalia to the value of US$6.7 million (European Commission 2014). Despite the enormous contributions of the APF, there have also been distinct limitations associated with this mechanism. As the APF is funded through the European Development Fund (EDF) under the Cotonou Agreement, military expenditures under the mechanism are restricted. The APF can be used to finance costs incurred by African countries in deploying their personnel to peace operations (which includes per diems, rations, medical consumables and facilities, transport, fuel, troop allowances and communication equipment), but it cannot be used to finance ammunition, arms, specific military equipment, salaries for troops and military training for soldiers. Accordingly, these kinds of expenditures have had to be funded through other means, in most cases usually through bilateral contributions from EU member states outside of the framework of the APF and the EDF (Pirozzi and Miranda 2010: 28). In addition, the contributions of the APF are limited, and are not necessarily able to meet all the funding requirements of African operations. As such, they are largely seen as a supporting financial measure, as opposed to the only financial mechanism, for African peace operations. Finally, it is not clear whether the APF can be funded through the EDF indefinitely, as the EDF funds are essentially development funds, which are not intended to finance peace operations. As such, additional mechanisms other than the APF, which has for a long time been the sole means of financing African operations, will need to be found going forward. Increasingly, however, it does seem that more complementary models of financing are evolving.

A significant development took place in January 2013, when the AU member states decided to contribute US$50 million to the organization's intervention in Mali, the first time that AU member states had made a financial contribution to the budget of a peace operation. Importantly, several means of sourcing these funds, in line with the PSC Protocol, were used, with US$20 million generated from arrear contributions, US$25 million from assessed funding, and US$5 million from the Peace Fund. Of this total amount, US$45 million was directed towards the AFISMA budget (which totalled an estimated US$460 million), and US$5 million towards the Malian Security and Defence Forces (MDSF) (African Union 2013a). Perhaps on the basis of this precedent, and recognizing that operations could no longer be fully funded by partners, African states in January 2015 decided to consider contributing 25 per cent of the African peace operations budget on a standing basis. Although no final decision on this matter was taken during the January 2015 summit, the AU Ad-hoc Ministerial Committee on the Scale of Assessment was requested to pursue consultations and propose modalities for the implementation of these and other financial measures, and to provide a report with recommendations at the next summit in June 2015 (African Union 2015). At the next summit in June 2015, and based on the work of the Ad-hoc Committee, AU member states took the decision to contribute 25 per cent of the budget of AU peace support operations, on an assessed scale, to be phased in over a period of five years. This represents the single most significant step ever taken by African states towards the funding of their own peace support operations to date.

Conclusion and way forward

To date, the development of frameworks, systems and procedures for the effective and efficient planning and delivery of support for African peace operations has been ad hoc and inconsistent, resulting in the development of four broad models of support which are heavily reliant on partner support, and which do not enable the AU or the RECs/RMs to independently plan, deploy and sustain their operations in the field. While the development of sustainable financial mechanisms to support such operations has also been slow to get off the ground, more progress has been attained here through the development of the EU APF, which provides a somewhat predictable framework for financing peace operations. In addition, the increased focus on the development of sustainable funding modalities by the AU, which commenced in early 2015, may also lead to interesting, and important, developments going forward, with the modalities of the June 2015 decision on assessed contributions from AU member states now requiring implementation.

However, addressing the question of sustainable funding will not be sufficient to strengthen African peace operations going forward. What will also be critically required is the development and operationalization of a functioning mission support concept and mechanisms for African peace operations. At present, operations are planned and personnel deployed into high-risk environments, and then whatever support is available, depending on the political dynamics at the time, is directed towards the mission. In a situation where in 2013 over 40,000 personnel were deployed in four African peace operations deployed in volatile situations, with combined budgets of close to US$2 billion for the year, this situation is less than ideal. Sufficient experience has been gained through the deployment of six major operations over the course of the past ten years, operating on the basis of four broad models of support which have been developed to date, to take stock of the lessons learned, and to strengthen African operations going forward.

This was echoed by the Independent Panel of Experts conducting the review of the ASF in 2013. In its report, the Panel noted that mission support was the least developed area of the ASF, and as this was a critical enabler for ASF operations, this had serious implications for the attainment of the full operating capability of the force. The Panel further found that the AU and the RECs/RMs had limited experience in the area of mission support, as partners had always taken responsibility for this aspect of the mission's work in the past. Overall, the Panel recommended an urgent reconceptualization of mission support for the ASF, and the prioritization of efforts to develop effective and efficient mechanisms that could meet the support requirements of African peace operations (African Union 2013b).

On this basis, the Panel specifically recommended that the AU Commission undertake a lessons-learned project aimed at capturing the key mission support lessons learned from peace operations to date, so that these could inform the revision and expansion of the ASF mission support concept. Specifically, the Panel recommended that the ASF mission support concept be reviewed and expanded to identify (1) the human resources required at the level of the planning elements, (2) the systems, structures and procedures the AU Commission and the RECs/RMs needed to develop, in addition to those that may already exist, and (3) the kind of stocks of equipment needed to be kept in strategic reserve, or for which just-in-time procurement contracts and arrangements needed to be established. On this note, the Panel recommended that the AU and the RECs/RMs move to a just-in-time procurement model that relies on pre-approved but dormant contracts in the areas of strategic lift, stocks and equipment that may be needed for mission start-up. Where it was deemed necessary to maintain stocks on a standby basis, such as, for instance, in relation to strategic communications equipment, the Panel recommended that the AU enter into negotiations with the UN to make use of its logistical depot in Kampala, Uganda, as opposed to developing its own continental and regional logistics bases.

The Panel further recommended that the AU Commission develop a lead nation support concept to enable rapid deployment in the context of specific interventions. On strategic lift, the Panel also recommended that the AU Commission and the RECs/RMs enter into pre-negotiated just-in-time contracts with service providers, as opposed to relying exclusively on the capacity of member states to undertake this. Finally, the Panel recommended that the AU Commission and the RECs/RMs invest in strategic and operational communication and information systems to enhance command and control of operations (ibid.: 11).

The implementation of the recommendations of the Panel will be important for the development of a mission support approach for African peace operations. However, the most important first steps which the AU and the RECs/RMs can take will be two specific ones. First, the AU and the RECs/RMs should conduct a comprehensive review of the lessons which have been learned in relation to mission support over the course of the past decade, identifying the strengths and weaknesses of each of the approaches, or models, which have been used to date. Secondly, and based on the outcomes of the lessons-learned exercise, a mission support concept should be jointly developed by the AU Commission and the RECs/REMs which meets the requirements of current operations, could meet the anticipated requirements of future operations, clearly outlines the concept to be used and assigns roles and responsibilities at each level of engagement accordingly. Without these two steps being taken, it is quite likely that the provision of support to African peace operations will continue to be ad hoc and unpredictable going forward, weakening the ability of these operations to effectively deliver on their mandates, and further hindering the development of rapidly deployable peace support operations which can effectively be supported in the field.

References

African Union (n.d. a) *Concept of Logistics Support for the Rapid Deployment Capability (RDC) of the African Standby Force (ASF)*, Unpublished.
— (n.d. b) *Draft Mission Support Concept for African Standby Force (ASF) Peace Support Operations*, Unpublished.
— (2002) *Protocol Relating to the Establishment of the Peace and Security Council of the African Union*, Durban: African Union, www.peaceau.org/uploads/psc-protocol-en.pdf, accessed 18 November 2015.
— (2003) *Policy Framework for the Establishment of the African Standby Force and the Military Staff Committee*, Addis Ababa: African Union, http://www.peaceau.org/uploads/asf-policy-framework-en.pdf, accessed 18 November 2015.
— (2013) *Solemn Declaration of the Assembly of the Union on the Situation in Mali*, Addis Ababa: African Union, www.issafrica.org/uploads/20th_Assembly_of_AU_Decisions_and_Declarations.pdf, accessed 18 November 2015.

— (2013b) *Report of the Independent Panel of Experts, Assessment of the African Standby Force and Plan of Action for achieving full operational capability by 2015*, Addis Ababa: African Union, Unpublished.
— (2014) *AU ASF and PSO Support Manual* (final version), Unpublished.
— (2015) *Decisions, Declarations and Resolutions of the Twenty-Fourth Ordinary Session of the Assembly of the Union – Decision on the Report of Alternative Sources of Financing the African Union (Doc.Assembly/AU/6(XXIV)*, Addis Ababa: African Union, summits.au.int/en/sites/default/files/Assembly%20AU%20Dec%20546%20-%20568%20%28XXIV%29%20_E.pdf.
European Commission (2014) *Factsheet – EU–Africa Relations*, Brussels: European Commission, europa.eu/rapid/press-release_MEMO-14-246_en.htm, accessed 18 November 2015.
Gelot, L., L. Gelot and C. de Coning (2012) *Supporting African Peace Operations*, Uppsala: Nordic Africa

Institute, nai.diva-portal.org/smash/
get/diva2:559425/FULLTEXT01.pdf.

Pirozzi, N. and V. Miranda (2010)
*Consolidating African and EU
Assessments in View of the
Implementation of the Partnership on*
Peace and Security, Rome: Istituto
Affari Internazionali, http://www.iai.
it/sites/default/files/consolidating-
african-and-eu-assessments.pdf,
accessed 18 November 2015.

7 | United in challenges? The African Standby Force and the African Capacity for the Immediate Response to Crises

Jide Martyns Okeke

Introduction

The last decade has witnessed an African renaissance in the response to crisis on the continent. Unlike in the Cold War and immediate post-Cold War years, when external actors primarily dictated solutions to conflicts on the continent, African actors are recognized as important partners in prevention of and response to crises in Africa. The deployments of African-led peace operations have been one of the most concrete, visible and prominent forms of African response to crisis situations on the continent. Between 2003 and 2015, African organizations – broadly defined in terms of the African Union (AU) and RECs/RMs – have deployed approximately 100,000 uniformed and civilian personnel in various theatres of operation. While this pattern of deployment may not necessarily reflect the dwindling number of conflicts in Africa in general, it represents two important trends. The first is the growing shift from 'saving strangers', which was based on the dominance of international response to the crisis in Africa, to a prominence of 'saving neighbours', defined in terms of the pursuit of regional collective security by African states (Okeke 2014; Williams and Dersso 2015). In addition, as the chapters by Aning & Abdallah (Chapter 2) and Dersso (Chapter 3) in this volume show, the unusual or unconventional nature of the security threats on the continent, characterized more by terrorist-related violence and transnational challenges and crime, have not necessarily been compatible with the traditional forms of peacekeeping missions, including under the Chapter VII provision. Rather, the use of force to regain territory and maintain state authority has been the norm in the practices of African-led peace operations. Despite the long-standing experience of the UN in peacekeeping missions, these have typically not been configured to respond to these forms of security threat in Africa, increasingly requiring combat operations akin to war fighting.

The second trend is related to the development of a normative and institutional framework to respond to crisis on the continent. In this regard, since the establishment of the AU, there has been a marked reconfiguration of the interventionist posture of African states, as reflected in various legal documents but also in the gains achieved in the development of the APSA. It is within the APSA framework that efforts have been made to respond to crisis through the deployment of peace operations but also through an institutionalized process based on the establishment of the ASF and its RDC. Efforts have been made to achieve the full operationalization of the ASF RDC, but the ambition of achieving a full operational capability (FOC) of this mechanism has not been realized. It is incontrovertible that the practices of African-led peace operations have benefited heavily from the ASF doctrine as well as from the process of capacity-building developed from the ASF RDC, but structured linkages and alignment between recent or current operations and the ASF RDC have never been made. As a result, concerns have been raised that the ASF RDC remains a work in progress and has prevented the continent from rapidly responding to crisis, which has sometimes allowed for external intervention to provide first responders. The case of the crisis in Mali has been cited as illustrative of this problem. This is why AU member states decided to establish the ACIRC as a transitional arrangement for rapid intervention, pending the full operationalization of the ASF RDC.

This chapter provides a review of efforts towards achieving FOC of the ASF RDC and its linkages with the ACIRC as a transitional mechanism. Three main observations are made: the first is that there has been progress towards attaining FOC of the ASF RDC but it is unlikely that the deadline of 2015 will be feasible to meet such an objective, given the gaps in the implementation of the Plan of Action submitted by the Independent Panel of Experts on the ASF. The second observation is that the ACIRC is promising because theoretically it represents, in concrete terms, African solutions to African problems with the utilization of largely continental resources. It has made significant progress towards attaining operational readiness since it was established just two years ago. However, the third observation made in this chapter is that both the ASF RDC and the ACIRC appear to be facing the same challenges to mechanisms to allow for rapid intervention. The process of mandating rapid deployment through international and regional decision-making organs, and the legal arrangements that will allow for pre-emptive commitments of AU member states to deploy their pledged capacities and the resources (both financial and in-kind contributions) are challenges that continue to adversely affect the prospects for African-led rapid deployment. If these challenges are not resolved, it will be almost impossible for either the ASF RDC or the ACIRC to undertake rapid intervention as envisaged by African actors.

The 'new' peace and security landscape in Africa

In the last decade there have been two important developments in the security landscape of Africa. The first is the changed or changing nature of security threats in Africa. The post-Cold War period, as commonly observed,

has been characterized by increased intra-state conflicts on the continent associated with struggles and contestations over resources, and ethnic/clan divisions
manifesting as religious tensions. This pattern of conflicts has been termed
'new' wars (Kaldor 1999) and has also been linked to the crisis of the state
in Africa associated with governance deficit and the inability of the state to
provide public goods (Allen 1999). Associated with the 'new' wars discourse is
the rising prominence of transnational criminal networks and terrorist groups
in Africa, as borne out by the discussion in Aning & Abdallah (Chapter 2) in
this volume. In some African states, territorial sovereignty has been challenged
owing to the inability of government to extend its authority across some territories. As both a cause and consequence, transnational criminal networks have
taken advantage of the vacuum to promote alternatively governed spaces for
the illicit trafficking of drugs, human trafficking and other forms of organized
crime. In addition, terrorist groups have managed to challenge state authority
by spreading radical Islamist ideology as well as wielding control over territories
and populations. The sustained influence of al-Shabaab in Somalia, the National
Movement for the Liberation of the Azawad (MNLA) and other armed groups
in northern Mali and the Boko Haram in north-eastern Nigeria and its spread
to Niger and Cameroon are cases in point. This pattern of unconventional
security threats does not detract from the progress that Africa continues to
make in macroeconomic and to a lesser extent microeconomic indicators in
several African states.

The second discernible pattern in Africa's peace and security landscape is
the rising prominence and recognition of intra-African responses. Since the
establishment of the AU in 2002, there has been a legal and institutional
transformation in the response to crisis in Africa. As an attempt to promote
renewed pan-Africanism and African renaissance, sometimes referred to as
'African solutions to African problems', the AU has embraced the principle
of non-indifference in crisis situations in Africa. This role of the AU as a
regional organization in the promotion of peace and security is provided for
in Chapter VIII of the UN Charter. In addition, the various legal provisions
of the AU, such as its Constitutive Act and the Protocol Establishing the Peace
and Security Council, are indicative of the transformative shift in the regional
collective security arrangements of African states from absolute sovereignty,
focused on regime security, to a redefinition of sovereignty as responsibility,
defined in terms of a primary focus on protection of civilians by the government (Deng 1996). There has also been an institutional reconfiguration of the
AU so that it can prevent and effectively respond to crisis situations through
the comprehensive APSA.

Efforts have been made towards the attainment of full operational capability (FOC) of the ASF since 2003. The indicators and requirements for achieving FOC have remained unclear, sometimes characterized by varied and not necessarily reinforcing conceptualizations on the part of various stakeholders. For instance, the 2013 Independent Panel of Experts on the Assessment of the ASF led by Professor Ibrahim Gambari provided three main benchmarks for understanding the idea of FOC for the ASF (African Union 2013). First is the ability of the AU Commission to mandate, plan, manage, support and liquidate a peace operation at the strategic level. This means that the AU Commission, working in a system-wide manner through the Peace Support Operations Division, should be able to coordinate the overall cycle for deploying a peace operation. Secondly, the AU Commission, or a designated REC/RM, should be able to plan, deploy, manage and support a peace operation at the operational level. The Protocol establishing the PSC of the AU designates RECs/RMs as implementing organs of the ASF, which means that the Strategic HQ of the ASF located within the AU Commission would have to rely on the capabilities of the regions to deploy peace operations. The third indicator is the ability of AU member states to generate the necessary military, police and civilian capabilities for the deployment of the ASF. In this section, the focus is on understanding the scope, operational requirements, including the prospects for rapid deployment, progress made and challenges encountered in achieving FOC for the ASF (ibid.).

The scope of the ASF is derived from, and premised on, the promotion of human security, through the capacity for preventing and responding to crisis situations. In this regard, the ASF is expected to support the PSC in the area of the deployment of peace operations and in cases of intervention defined in terms of Article 4(h) and (j) respectively. This scope has been delineated in terms of six scenarios that range from mere military observation (scenario 1) to a robust intervention in prevention of, or in response to, imminent gross human rights violations (genocide, war crimes and crimes against humanity) (scenario 6). In terms of the operational requirements for the deployment of the ASF, there are four main considerations that must be taken into account.[1] The first is the mandating authority for the deployment of the ASF. The PSC remains the primary decision-making organ for the deployment of the ASF for the purposes of consensual peace operations, with the consent of the host country. In cases where there is a need for intervention without the consent of the host state, to avert or respond to mass atrocities, the AU Assembly remains the exclusive authority authorizing the ASF. Specifically, it is required that there must be a two-thirds majority vote in favour of such an intervention. To date, there has not been any intervention by AU member states under the Article

4(h) provision, which may be linked to the difficulty of achieving a timely quorum as well as consensus among the fifty-four member states of the Union. Beyond the PSC and the Assembly, the RECs/RMs and national legislatures possess the authority for the deployment of the ASF. While this is not taken into account within the Protocol, it remains a very important dimension for achieving timely deployment. For example, there may be significant delays in deploying an African-mandated peace operation if there are difficulties in getting an endorsement from the relevant REC/RM as well as national authorities for the employment of regional capabilities.

The second operational requirement is the readiness of the planning elements (PLANELMs). The PLANELMs are the required capabilities established at both the AU Commission and the RECs/RMs responsible for the planning, deployment, management and liquidation of peace operations. The AU PSOD is the PLANELM at the strategic level located within the AU Commission in Addis Ababa, while the regions are often regarded as the operational PLANELMs. This is not, however, fixed, because it is possible for regional PLANELMs to be temporarily transformed into a strategic authority if there is a deployment by a subregional organization that may not be officially recognized by the AU. For example, the Lake Chad Basin Commission (LCBC), currently playing an important role in the fight against Boko Haram through the establishment of the Multinational Joint Task Force (MNJTF), may be regarded as an operational HQ, while a region such as the Economic Community of West African States (ECOWAS) could be referred to as a strategic HQ if it has command and control responsibility over LCBC. There have been efforts made towards the development of the AU PSOD as a strategic HQ over the last decade. It has managed to increase its capacity to deploy multidimensional and integrated missions through the recruitment and mainstreaming of civilians, police and military across the Division. The experiences of deploying, managing and liquidating various peace operations have significantly enhanced the expertise of the AU PSOD. Yet the rotation of military personnel, over-reliance on external funding and limited police and civilian strength continue to challenge the institutionalization of best practices. The regional PLANELMs are also building their capacities for managing and liquidating peace operations, including through the secondment of AU PSOD staff to support the process of capacity-building (in the case of ECOWAS). Unfortunately, there are still gaps in the synergy, coordination and communication required to ensure standardized practices between the strategic and operational HQs of the ASF. This is further complicated by the absence of a legal framework between the AU and the regions on the employment of the ASF.

The third critical requirement is the availability of pledged capabilities. Member states are expected to pledge capabilities – for instance, contingents, equipment, individually deployed police officers (IPOs) and formed police units

(FPUs) as well as civilian expertise in support of the ASF. The initial conception of pledged capabilities as contained in the ASF Policy Framework was based on the assumption that pledged resources from member states would be standing, so that they can be readily available once needed. Increasingly, however, the notion of pledges for the ASF is being defined in terms of available capabilities that can be deployed by member states in support of a peace operation (African Union 2003). In this way, it would be possible for member states to provide capabilities based on availability rather than on equal provision of resources to the regions by member states. All the pledged capabilities should be verified on a periodic basis in order to ensure that they meet the required AU standards and compliance with international humanitarian and human rights laws. Unfortunately, such verification has not been undertaken for all the regional standby forces and it is uncertain whether the pledges made are commensurate with the capability that can be made available to the region, in cases of deployment of a peace operation.

The fourth operational requirement relates to mission support, and we know from Lotze's (Chapter 6) analysis in this volume that this critical area has been neglected to date. The ASF mission support concept is defined in terms of the critical enablers and multipliers, logistics and funding that must be put in place to allow for deployment and sustainment of a peace operation. The provision of this mission support requirement is expected to be the initial responsibility of national authorities of the pledged countries. Accordingly, the ASF doctrine requires that police- and troop-contributing countries are able to self-sustain for between thirty days (under scenarios 1–3) and sixty days (for scenarios 4–6), including in the provision of the required equipment (ibid.). The initial thinking was also to establish an ASF logistical depot for the reserves and stocks that may be employed in support of an ASF deployment. However, this idea has proved to be difficult to achieve, owing especially to the problem of maintaining assets that may become moribund during prolonged storage. Besides, the cost of maintaining a logistical depot may also be too high to sustain. As a result, Cedric de Coning (2014) has argued for a just-in-time model, which is based on the pre-contractual agreement with service providers, as a more contemporary approach to the static logistics depot model. In terms of funding the ASF, the Protocol provides for the establishment of the AU Peace Fund, with contributions from African states (both voluntary and assessed) as well as international partners. Article 21 of the Protocol stipulates that 'following a decision by the relevant Policy Organs of the Union, the cost of operations of the ASF shall be assessed by Member States based on the scale of their contributions to the regular budget of the Union' (African Union 2002). Despite this provision, the costs of peace operations have been primarily derived from contributions from international partners. This is due to the limited contributions, both assessed and voluntary, from AU member states. In other words, the practice of African peace operations may never have materialized without the current support packages, in terms of both financial support and in-kind contributions from core international partners, as detailed by Darkwa (Chapter 5) previously in this book. This challenge remains one of the most profound of the obstacles that continue to face the ASF.

These critical factors for the full operationalization of the ASF have been developed partly through a training exercise cycle known as the AMANI Africa Exercise, composed of both a command post exercise (CPX) and a field training exercise (FTX). In October 2010, a CPX was conducted focused mainly on validating policies and processes, at the continental strategic level, in employing the ASF. The Evaluation Report that emanated from this exercise concluded that the ASF had attained initial operational capability (IOC). However, it was determined that there was a need for a follow-up training cycle, which will provide for an opportunity to ensure greater multidimensionality across the civilian, police and military components as well as better interoperability between capabilities available in various regions for the ASF. It is against this background that Exercise NJIWA was launched in March 2012, to strengthen the police and civilian capacities of the ASF in the planning for and deployment of peace operations. The last phase of this exercise is the AMANI Africa II, consisting of further promotion of common understanding and streamlining of planning and decision-making processes, training for the strategic, operational and tactical headquarters and an FTX. All these activities, except for the FTX, took place in 2014, and the operational readiness of the ASF has been determined following the FTX, which took place in Lohatla, South Africa in October/November 2015. While the various training cycles do not primarily define the ASF, they form an important aspect in preparation for achieving the FOC of the ASF, expected by the end of 2015.

One of the most critical but often contentious areas regarding the deployment of the ASF is linked to the operationalization of its RDC. Under the ASF concept all regions should develop a rapid deployment element. This would require that states are able to make available the pledged capacities within a very short time frame, not exceeding thirty days, and in cases of imminent mass atrocities not more than fourteen days. For such a rapid deployment to succeed, there is a need for early establishment of an effective mission headquarters. This would require the development of a standby procedure similar to the SHIRBRIG concept (UN 2007).[2] Some RECs/RMs, such as the East African Standby Force Coordination Mechanism (EASFCOM), ECOWAS and the Economic Community of Central African States (ECCAS), have declared that their various standby forces have attained full operational capability, but it is the FTX that will provide the operational status of the ASF. Amid the prolonged and continued efforts to fully operationalize the ASF, a decision was made by the AU Assembly of Heads of State and Government to establish the ACIRC as an interim measure.

African Capacity for Immediate Response to Crises

It has been noted previously in this volume that while attempts are still being made to attain FOC of the ASF, the AU has led or coordinated several peace operations. Two main concerns have been expressed by AU member states about the emerging pattern of African-led peace operations. The first is that these deployments have not been framed in terms of or deployed as ASF operations. In other words, there have been parallel approaches in terms of the ambition to achieve FOC of the ASF and the establishment, management and liquidation of African peace operations. At the same time, some of these operations have significantly benefited from the processes and procedures that have been developed through the capacity-building programmes designed to support the regions in achieving the operational readiness of their respective standby forces. For example, the principles that have underpinned the deployment of African-led peace operations in Mali and Central African Republic in terms of planning, force generation, self-sustainment and liquidation or transition to a UN peacekeeping mission have been in accordance with the ASF doctrine. However, there has not been any structured or institutionalized pattern of relationship between the ASF and recent/current African-led peace operations. Aligning current operations with the ASF doctrine was identified by the 'Gambari Panel' as one of the concrete steps that can be undertaken by the AU in order to reinforce efforts towards FOC of the ASF by 2015. The second concern has been the timeliness of deployments during crisis situations. In this respect, it appears that African states, through the ASF, have not been able to deploy rapidly, thus sometimes allowing for extra-African interventions to provide first responders to the crisis. This was mainly identified in the case of the crisis in Mali, in which the French-led Opération Serval intervened to curb the growing challenge to state authority by the armed opposition groups in northern Mali.

These two concerns were expressed by the AU member states during the 20th Summit of Heads of States and Government, held in Addis Ababa, Ethiopia, in January 2013. As a result, the AU Assembly decided there was a need to undertake an assessment of the ASF in order to identify the challenges encountered, and to make concrete recommendations on how to ensure FOC of the ASF by 2015. This decision was further reiterated during the 6th Ordinary Meeting of the Specialized Technical Committee of Ministers of Defence, Safety and Security (STCDSS) held in Addis Ababa on 30 April 2013. Subsequently, a Panel of Experts was constituted by the AU Commission, led by Professor Ibrahim Gambari and Cedric de Coning, to undertake this assessment. This Panel determined that substantial progress had been made in efforts towards the operationalization of the ASF, especially in three main RECs/RMs, namely EASFCOM, ECOWAS and the Southern African Development Community (SADC). Nevertheless, the progress achieved could not translate into the attainment of FOC of the ASF by the end of 2015. Therefore, the Panel proposed a Plan of Action focused on specific areas that must be implemented ahead of December 2015, in order to achieve FOC. In addition, it proposed a collective verification process of pledged capabilities of regional standby forces, with the findings presented to the AU Assembly by January 2016 for a determination of whether the ASF has attained FOC.

After long and difficult deliberations, which potentially divided influential AU member states, the Assembly of Heads of States and Government agreed in principle during the 21st Summit, which took place in Addis Ababa in May 2013, to establish the ACIRC as a transitional arrangement, pending the full operationalization of the ASF. The establishment of the ACIRC was also supposed to be perceived as an expression of a renewed sense of African solidarity and political will because it coincided with the celebration of the fiftieth anniversary of the establishment of the Organization of African Unity (OAU) as well as celebration of a decade of the AU. The remainder of this section focuses on the underlying principles, operational concepts, concrete achievements and outstanding gaps of the ACIRC.

Since the adoption of the decision by the AU to establish the ACIRC, questions have been raised on how this mechanism differs from the RDC of the ASF. There are five core principles of the ACIRC that suggest points of departure from the ASF and its RDC. The first is that the ACIRC is underpinned by the principle of continental voluntarism, wherein AU member states, based on their respective capacities, wilfully decide to make contributions towards fulfilling the requirements that would allow for rapid deployment. By so doing, pledged capabilities made to the regions by states will also be made available to ACIRC Volunteering Nations, to allow for rapid deployment. However, there is no current legal agreement that stipulates that these regional pledges can be made available outside of the command and control structure of the regional standby forces. Secondly, the ACIRC is supposed to operate based on the principle of flexibility, which allows for the standardization of equipment to be defined not in terms of uniformity, as associated with the ASF RDC, but rather in terms of capacity to deliver. Therefore, the standard table of equipment (ToE) and standardized training are defined in terms of the minimal requirements that will allow for efficiency when the ACIRC is deployed. The rationale for such a minimalist approach is to overcome the often high standards set by the ASF RDC as well as the UN in absorbing troops for rapid deployments.

Thirdly, there is a redefinition of the notion of self-sustainment under the ACIRC arrangement, in the following ways. The overall timeline for deployment of the ACIRC is envisaged as not exceeding ninety days, the costs of which should be borne by the Volunteering Nations. The reimbursement of the costs of such an operation by the AU will only be for sixty days, and will be made only six months following the end of an operation. Following operational planning towards achieving readiness of the ACIRC, the AU Commission has determined that the total cost for a ninety-day operation will be approximately US$57 million, including strategic lift. The AU Commission will be responsible for common costs associated with an ACIRC operation, meaning, for instance, the establishment of a force HQ, strategic lift and out-of-theatre support elements such as medical services (African Union 2014). Some Volunteering Nations have, however, pledged to cover some of these common expenditures such as strategic lift, meaning that the estimated total cost of an ACIRC operation could be substantially reduced. Fourthly, the ACIRC is based on an envisaged deployment timeline of forty-eight hours in cases of an intervention under Article 4(h) of the AU Constitutive Act. This is clearly much more ambitious than the fourteen-day timeline associated with the deployment of the RDC, in similar cases. The final characteristic of the ACIRC is the concept of Framework Nation, which means states that are able to facilitate the initial deployment through the establishment of the force HQ and other operational requirements for immediate deployment of the ACIRC. This is not exclusive to the ACIRC and is also provided for within the ASF RDC concept as well. The difference here is that the Framework Nations will be rotational on a three-month basis, whether or not there is an operation, across the Volunteering Nations.

The operational concept for the ACIRC has been conceived across three levels of operations: the first is related to tactical operations and involves six battalions that have been pledged by Angola, Chad, Niger, Uganda, Rwanda and South Africa. The second level will be the force HQ, which will be allocated to the Volunteering Nations on a rotational basis. The third level is the operational HQ, expected to be headed by a Special Envoy with some police and civilian elements, namely a humanitarian adviser, a civil–military coordination officer, a political adviser, a legal adviser and a police adviser. This operational HQ may be located outside of the theatre of ACIRC operation at the inception but will gradually be relocated to the area of responsibility as the security condition improves. Overall, the operational architecture of the ACIRC is built upon the securitization of civilian protection, premised on the need to undertake combat operations in order to achieve immediate stabilization rather than long-term promotion of an effective strategy for durable solutions to the crisis. The latter will be undertaken by other follow-on activities, including post-conflict reconstruction and development programmes by the AU in close collaboration with other relevant international organizations.

At the time of writing, only thirteen out of the fifty-four member states of the AU have volunteered to be part of the ACIRC, representing only 24 per cent of continental membership. These countries include Algeria, Angola, Burkina Faso, Chad, Ghana, Egypt, Niger, Senegal, Uganda, South Africa, the Sudan and Rwanda. Political crisis in countries like Burkina Faso and to some extent Egypt may continue to affect the initial commitments made by these countries. It is also interesting to observe that Ethiopia, which chaired the Assembly when the decision to establish the ACIRC was made and also committed to be part of this mechanism, and remains one of the world's largest troop-contributing countries, may have rescinded its support for it. The reasons for this changed position remain unclear but generally reflect the gaps that often exist between the political declarations made by AU member states during the AU summit and technical implementation, which in this case will be under the purview of the Ministry of Defence.

The ACIRC has been lauded for its achievements, given the short time frame in which it was established. An ACIRC PLANELM within the Peace Support Operations Division of the AU Commission in Addis Ababa has been established. In 2014, verification of pledged units and resources was also conducted in order to ascertain the operational readiness of Volunteering Nations. This seems to be a milestone, especially given that the AU Commission has not conducted a similar exercise for the ASF RDC. In November 2014, a CPX was also conducted in Dar es Salaam, Tanzania, to determine the operational readiness of the ACIRC. It must be noted that only nine out of the thirteen Volunteering Nations participated in this exercise but it involved 116 military personnel, with Uganda as the exercise director, South Africa as deputy exercise director and Angola as chief evaluator. Chad was the controller of the exercise while Tanzania acted as the force commander. The planned FTX for the AMANI Africa II exercise scheduled to take place in South Africa by September 2015 may include the ACIRC as part of harmonization efforts with the ASF RDC.

Harmony in the challenges confronting the ASF RDC and the ACIRC

There was initial tension regarding the establishment of the ACIRC in some states – for example, Nigeria and Cameroon – which argued that it could potentially create a parallel process that would distract the AU from efforts to ensure FOC of the ASF RDC. Some RECs/RMs, such as ECOWAS, ECCAS and EASFCOM, have remained highly critical of the ACIRC, because they were not consulted over and represented in its establishment and operationalization processes. In fact, some of these regions have made self-declarations on attaining FOC of their regional capabilities (for example, EASFCOM and ECCAS) or are seeking to establish a parallel regional mechanism for rapid deployment. In terms of the latter, the After Action Review by ECOWAS in its response to the crisis in Mali recommended the establishment of a special standby two-battalion rapid response force ready to intervene within thirty days of any complex emergency in West Africa. The review also proposed the signing of Memoranda of Understanding with its ECOWAS member states for the provision of standing units to a regional standby force, which would be self-sustaining for the first ninety days of deployment (ECOWAS 2014).

As part of efforts to resolve this challenge, the STCDSS, during its seventh meeting held on 14 January 2014 in Addis Ababa, recommended that both the ACIRC and RDC concepts should be harmonized to avoid duplication of efforts and ensure that the ACIRC assists in expediting the operationalization process of the RDC. The STCDSS declaration also emphasized that the ACIRC initiative should be captured as a phase in the implementation roadmap and operationalization of the ASF, including its RDC. These recommendations were in accordance with the decision of the AU Assembly of Heads of States and Government on the establishment of the ACIRC as a transitional arrangement, adopted during the 21st Summit held in May 2014.

In Addis Ababa, the process of harmonization seems to have commenced, with the development of a revised Consolidated Roadmap on the ACIRC and the ASF. In this regard, the ACIRC is seen as a catalyst for the RDC because Volunteering Nations are pledging the same capacities towards both the ASF and the ACIRC. The Consolidated Roadmap has also identified a number of relevant activities – for example, the convening of a workshop to discuss areas of commonalities between the RDC and the ACIRC involving the regions; development of plans and modalities for merging both the RDC and the ACIRC; and a technical experts' meeting to interrogate the attainment of FOC for both the RDC and the ACIRC. Unfortunately, these activities have not been implemented as scheduled. However, it has been observed that the CPX scenario for the ACIRC was similar to the ASF RDC concept and therefore bears a resemblance to the envisaged process of harmonization. As previously mentioned, the FTX of the ASF involved the ACIRC officers currently embedded in the AU PSOD in the planning and execution of this exercise. The ACIRC RDC was also deployed at the tactical level as part of the exercise.

Indeed, it appears that the discourse regarding and efforts towards harmonization have been dominated by unclear (and at worst deficient) technical mechanisms as regards both the ACIRC and the ASF RDC. However, the most profound and yet unresolved questions of harmonization are linked to political, legal and resource preconditions for rapid deployment, which are still unresolved both within the framework of the ACIRC as well as in the ASF RDC. The political consideration is linked to the mandating authority for rapid deployment. The authorization for rapid deployment based on the consent of the host state as provided for in Article 4(j) is quite clear and straightforward because it can be issued through the PSC. This does not preclude other levels of mandating authority at the UN and in regional and national constituencies. In fact, the Independent Panel of the ASF recognized these multiple levels of decision-making as a challenge for rapid deployment. Nonetheless, the practice of African-led peace operations has demonstrated that even though response to the crisis may not be rapid enough, there is a high likelihood of authorization by the PSC. The issue of mandating authority becomes much more complicated in situations requiring rapid intervention under the provision of Article 4(h). This would require the two-thirds majority vote by the AU Assembly of Heads of State and Government. Since the establishment of the AU, there has not been one single evocation of Article 4(h) owing to the politics of consensus among AU member states but also to the difficulty in achieving a quorum of heads of state and government within the short time frame needed to allow for a rapid deployment within two to fourteen days, as provided for in both the ASF RDC and the ACIRC. A proposal for the delegation of responsibility to the PSC as well as ACIRC Volunteering Nations for authorizing a rapid intervention was submitted to the AU Assembly during its 25th Summit held in Addis Ababa on 30/31 January 2015. However, this proposal was not considered by the AU member states.

The legal question that remains unaddressed relates to the legal arrangement between the AU and ACIRC Volunteering Nations as well as between the Volunteering Nations and non-Volunteering Nations. One of the challenges confronting the ASF RDC is the absence of a Memorandum of Understanding (MoU) between the AU and the regions on the employment of the ASF. Similarly, the AU Commission will have to sign MoUs with the ACIRC Volunteering Nations for the utilization of their capacities. This process has already commenced and if it succeeds will allow for a legally binding pre-commitment from ACIRC states for rapid deployment. The unresolved challenge is what legal arrangements will be put in place between the Volunteering Nations and non-Volunteering Nations in situations where transport assets (water, air, land) of the latter may be required. The limited inclusivity of AU member states in the ACIRC process suggests that this will present a huge challenge. The resource element also remains a potential problem. Unlike the ASF RDC, which has been almost exclusively funded by international partners, a unique feature of the ACIRC is the emphasis on African resources to address African problems. In this regard, beyond the self-sustainment principle applied to all ACIRC Volunteering Nations, other forms of support will be derived from assessed contributions of AU member states and in-kind contributions. If this is accepted by all AU member states given the limited ACIRC representation, the limited funds in the Peace Fund from assessed contributions will make it difficult to sustain an operation. Efforts by the AU to generate alternative sources of funding from within the continent have not yielded positive results, including through the Ministerial Committee led by Nigeria following the submission of the Report on the Alternative Sources of Funding by Olusegun Obasanjo. Besides, most of the ACIRC member states continue to rely heavily on bilateral assistance to boost military capacity, through such programmes as

Africa Contingency Operations Training Assistance (ACOTA) and the recently launched African Peacekeeping Rapid Response Partnership (A-PREP) initiative by the United States.

Overall, the ACIRC and the ASF RDC have increased the visibility and recognition of African states as important actors in Africa's peace and security landscape. At the same time, they have reinforced the perception of a growing militarization of peace in Africa, where the solution to crisis is almost entirely dependent on the use of force. As a result, alternative forms of peacemaking and the need to strengthen conflict prevention strategies have not received as much attention. This is a clear gap in the practice of the APSA and does not address the quest for sustainable peace in Africa. Even the so-called rapid development mechanisms continue to face serious difficulties in the common understanding of the scope, vision and overall end-state of this endeavour. Without clarity in the political, legal and resource preconditions for rapid deployment, both the ASF RDC and the ACIRC will continue to be united in facing the challenges of timely response rather than become contenders to provide such a response.

Conclusion

Africa will continue to define, influence and be part of the developments in the peace and security sphere on the continent. The growing institutionalization of Africa's role through the AU and its APSA reaffirms the regionalization of peace in Africa. At the same time, there seems to be an emphasis on hard-security approaches that tends to privilege the militarization of peace as a solution for stabilization. The operationalization of the ASF RDC and the establishment of the ACIRC as a transitional mechanism are illustrative of this approach. The ASF RDC continues to be a work in progress even a decade since it was first conceived, with uncertainty around whether it will ever achieve FOC. The ACIRC, on the other hand, is a transitional arrangement which, despite its promises, has been perceived as being in competition with, or attempting to replace the gains already made by, the ASF RDC. As this chapter demonstrates, neither mechanism can be sufficient for rapid develop-ment if the traditional problems of political mandate, legal arrangements and resources are not addressed.

Notes

1 These indicators are anchored in the framework adopted by the Independent Panel of Experts on the Assessment of the ASF and therefore provide a generic basis for assessing the ASF, which may not be universally accepted by all relevant stakeholders.

2 The Multinational Standby High Readiness Brigade for United Nations Operations (SHIRBRIG) was developed in 1996 and is a multinational brigade that can be made available to the UN as a rapidly deployable peacekeeping force. See UN (2007).

References

African Union (2002) *Protocol Relating to the Establishment of the Peace and Security Council of the African Union*, Durban: African Union, www.peaceau.org/uploads/psc-protocol-en.pdf, accessed 18 November 2015.

— (2003) *Policy Framework for the Establishment of the African Standby Force and the Military Staff Committee*, Addis Ababa: African Union, http://www.peaceau.org/uploads/asf-policy-framework-en.pdf, accessed 18 November 2015.

— (2013) *Report of the Independent Panel of Experts, Assessment of the African Standby Force and Plan of Action for achieving full operational capability by 2015*, Addis Ababa: African Union, Unpublished.

— (2014) *The Report of the CPX for the ACIRC*, Addis Ababa: African Union, Unpublished.

Allen, C. (1999) 'Warfare, endemic violence, and state collapse in Africa', *Review of African Political Economy*, XXVI(81): 367–84.

De Coning, C. (2014) 'Enhancing the efficiency of the ASF: the case for a shift to a just-in-time rapid response model', *Conflict Trends*, 2: 34–40.

Deng, F. M. (1996) *Sovereignty as Responsibility: Conflict Management in Africa*, Washington, DC: Brookings Institution.

ECOWAS (2014) 'Experts call for an effective ECOWAS Standby Force', Press release, 8 February, news.ecowas.int/presseshow.php?nb=013&lang=en&annee=2014, accessed 15 January 2015.

Kaldor, M. (1999) *New and Old Wars: Organized Violence in a Global Era*, Cambridge: Polity Press.

Okeke, J. M. (2014) 'An evolving model of African-led peace support operations: lessons from Burundi, Sudan (Darfur) and Somalia', in T. Tardy and M. Wyss (eds), *Peacekeeping in Africa: The Evolving Security Architecture*, New York: Routledge.

UN (United Nations) (2007) *SHIRBRIG: Ready to deploy*, United Nations, http://www.un.org/en/peacekeeping/publications/yir/2006/shirbrig.htm, accessed 18 November 2015.

Williams, P. D. and S. A. Dersso (2015) *Saving Strangers and Neighbors: Advancing UN–AU Cooperation on Peace Operations*, New York: International Peace Institute, www.ipinst.org/wp-content/uploads/2015/02/IPI-E-pub-Saving-Strangers-and-Neighbors.pdf, accessed 18 November 2015.

8 | What roles for the civilian and police dimensions in African peace operations?

Yvonne Akpasom

Introduction

When the ASF was conceptualized in the early 2000s, an important determinant for its success was the requirement for multidimensionality, which was deemed necessary for addressing the comprehensive set of needs of countries as they transition from conflict to peace. Although the initial efforts to establish the ASF were focused heavily on the military component of the force, from 2006 onwards efforts were also expended to further develop the police and civilian components thereof. In this regard, numerous policy frameworks were developed, and, specifically on the civilian side, guidance was established that would inform the staffing, training, rostering and recruitment needs for the effective integration of civilians in missions.

In recent times, there has been some uncertainty about the need for multidimensional capacities in African operations. The development of new initiatives – for example, the ACIRC – has, as the chapter by Jide Okeke (Chapter 7) in this volume engages with in depth, stirred concerns among some that there is an attempt to militarize African missions. Others still have questioned the capacity of the AU and the RECs/RMs to deploy civilian and police personnel and whether in so doing they run the risk of duplicating important roles in this regard as undertaken by, in particular, the UN.

The reality, however, as evidenced in recent experiences of the AU in peace operations mounted in Somalia, Mali and the CAR, is that there does not seem to be a narrowing presence of civilian and police personnel in these missions as the very mandates they are called upon to implement go beyond what is obtainable through the exclusive employment of military capacities and capabilities. Apart from this, very few today would dispute the conventional wisdom that military solutions alone are inadequate for addressing, in the long term, the systemic causes of conflict.

Thus, it is not so much a question of whether or not the AU should invest in military capacities alone, but rather of having a forward-looking outlook on the role of the AU. Granted, the UN has a significant wealth of accumulated experience and the organization is optimally positioned to deploy and sustain elaborate multidimensional capacities. But there is a role for the AU in this regard as well, though it need not be expansive. The AU should identify areas where it has a comparative advantage or areas of work wherein it stands to achieve the most impact, and in turn it should continue to be supported in its efforts.

This chapter therefore serves to highlight the continued relevance of multidimensionality in African peace operations. It also reflects on recent experiences in this regard and draws out some key areas that will need to be addressed to strengthen the multidimensional approach.

A trend towards the militarization of African peace operations?

Among some observers there is a floating perception of or concern about a noticeable trend towards an increased militarization of African peace operations, and several indications have been cited in this regard, not least of which is the recent decision by the AU Commission (AUC) to establish the ACIRC (African Union 2013a). The ACIRC has been constructed as a *strictly military capacity*, contingent on military capabilities, force multipliers and resources from within the continent. Its envisaged roles include stabilization, peace enforcement and intervention missions; the neutralization of terrorist groups, cross-border criminal entities and armed rebellions; and emergency assistance to member states. There have been several dilemmas and controversies presented by the ACIRC, one of which is the implications it has, going forward, for the multidisciplinary and multidimensional imperative of African peace operations, given that it lacks any civilian, police or specialized non-military components, all of which are ultimately important in the consolidation of long-term peace and stability.

Indeed, the ACIRC stands in stark contrast to the ASF vision and concept. Article 13 of the AU PSC Protocol outlines the establishment of a multidimensional mechanism comprising civilian and military components,[1] held on standby in their countries of origin, ready for rapid deployment at appropriate notice. The Protocol further directs the AU to establish and centrally manage a roster of 'mission administration' and 'civilian experts' to handle human rights, humanitarian, governance, reconstruction and DDR functions in future missions. The PSC Protocol, Article 13(3), provides for several mission scenarios which include, among others, 'intervention in a Member State in respect of grave circumstances or at the request of a Member State in order to restore peace and security' and 'peace-building, including post-conflict disarmament and demobilization'. This implies, then, that ASF missions may be entrusted to undertake a multiplicity of activities with profoundly political consequences that cover the full gamut of conflict prevention, management, resolution, peacekeeping and post-conflict reconstruction and development.

When it comes to the question of whether the ACIRC is an indicator of increased militarization of peace operations in Africa, perhaps a cautious approach should be adopted. As stated by the chairperson of the AU Commission, the ACIRC is intended as an *interim* measure pending the full operationalization of the ASF and the RDC, and will serve as a robust and credible force that is deployable over a minimum duration of time to address specific goals (African Union 2013b). Additionally, AU member states directed that efforts to establish the ACIRC should be harmonized with efforts to establish the ASF and its RDC – though in practice there have been some challenges in ensuring appropriate linkages between the two at the level of the AUC. Thus, the ACIRC is at least on a surface evaluation not intended to become a permanent solution, and even if it tried, it would likely fail in the long run given that conventional wisdom suggests that the effective management and resolution of conflict are necessarily dependent on political direction and solutions.

Additionally, there have in essence been no official pronouncements to date by the AU member states that reflect a complete abandonment of the ASF vision in its broadest articulation. If we move forward from here on the assumption that the ASF vision is still alive, albeit in need of some important reinforcement and/or modification of the concept to ensure its viability in the long run, then multidimensionality will remain an important characteristic of African peace operations going forward.

Furthermore, purely militaristic approaches to conflict management are also foolhardy when considered against the challenges presented by instability and crisis on the continent. Conflict has generated a number of effects, including widespread loss of life and property, gross violations of human rights, especially for vulnerable groups, large-scale displacement of populations as they try to flee from violence, and, in the process, the disruption of livelihoods and society. The human effect of these various threats has led to a shift from a more state-centric concept of security to a people-centric concept which places emphasis on meeting basic needs and aspirations. The continent is also faced with a growing number of emerging or non-traditional transnational security threats and challenges, including asymmetrical warfare and terrorism, maritime insecurity and transnational organized crime, as we have seen in the chapter by Aning & Abdallah in this volume (Chapter 2). Additionally, in many conflict scenarios across the continent, we find a decimation of state institutions as concerns, for example, the rule of law, security and justice. A net consequence, then, is that security has increasingly become tied to concerns that transcend hard military-security issues to include issues of governance, rule of law, democracy, human rights and development.

Within the context of the wider instruments and processes of the APSA, robust and effective peace operations will remain an important way in which the consequences of these threats are contained and/or managed. An increased possibility of the attainment of durable peace will necessarily be contingent on operations that are multidimensional, bringing together contributions from both uniformed and non-uniformed personnel. Having said this, it is important to note that while peace operations will likely remain an important strategic tool, in the African context, we need to pay attention also to how we can better achieve an optimum operationalization of all the elements of the APSA and to sharpen our responses insofar as conflict prevention and early warning are concerned.

Towards a fit-for-purpose approach in addressing complex crises

The mandates provided to recent AU peace operations, including those deployed to Somalia, Mali and the CAR, support the assertion of multidimensionality as a prevalent feature of African peace operations. AU missions now typically employ a civilian-led multidimensional mission management structure with military, police and civilian substantive and support components. Mandates have become increasingly multifaceted and, needless to say, ambitious, directing missions to support, among other elements, national authorities in reducing the threats posed by belligerent groups; national authorities in their primary responsibility to protect civilian populations; political transition and dialogue processes; monitoring of human rights situations and promotion of and respect for fundamental rights and freedoms; consolidation and restoration of state authority; effective re-establishment of police forces; disarmament processes and measures designed to strengthen the security sector and the rule of law; stabilization and post-conflict reconstruction efforts; and the creation of conditions conducive to the delivery of humanitarian assistance.

In support of these mandated tasks, the number of police and civilians in AU missions has over the years increased both in quantitative and qualitative terms. While the AU Mission in Burundi has approximately twenty-five international staff, the AU Mission in Somalia (AMISOM) presently has an authorized strength of seventy civilians; the African-led International Support Mission to Mali (AFISMA) was authorized with 173 civilians, including fifty human rights observers; and the African-led International Support Mission to the CAR (MISCA) was authorized with a strength of 152 civilians. Present considerations for civilian staffing in the MNJTF against Boko Haram include 150 civilian personnel. The areas in which these operatives function in the various missions include political and civil affairs, protection, human rights and gender, public information and humanitarian liaison and conduct and discipline, among others. In addition to these substantive functions, civilian personnel also play an important support function in the areas of finance, human resources, procurement and information technology, and so forth.

These figures are relatively small as compared to civilian staffing numbers in United Nations missions, and deliberately so, based on two key assumptions that have guided the development of the civilian dimension of African operations over the past ten years. The first is that there would be financing constraints for the foreseeable future for these operations until such time as sustainable funding mechanisms could be identified. As such, planning for civilian staffing in African operations would have to take a conservative approach, necessitating fewer, more broadly functioning staff. Current African missions have therefore adopted an approach wherein cross-cutting functions have been concentrated into single units – thus, for example, a Protection, Human Rights and Gender Unit or a Political and Civilian Affairs Unit. A second key assumption is that African operations would predominantly take on stability operations for a limited duration, followed by a UN operation that would undertake a longer-term peacebuilding role (De Coning and Kasumba 2010: 65). This trend has been the case, for instance, in the context of Mali and the CAR.

The role of police in African operations has also received increased focus over the last decade, and police have been tasked with responsibilities (among others) in supporting long-term capacity-building and development (through co-location, strategic advisory support for police reform, operational mentoring, multidisciplinary training), law enforcement and public order management, operational capabilities of host country police and other law enforcement officials, as well as providing reassurance in the areas of public safety and the security of communities (African Union 2014a: 2). As at January 2014, in what is the largest peace operation globally, the AMISOM police component comprised a relatively modest 517 police officers, including 279 formed police units (FPUs) and 233 individual police officers (IPOs) tasked with training, mentoring and advising the Somali Police Force (SPF) on aspects including human rights observation, crime prevention strategies and community policing and search procedures and investigations, as well as providing support to the federal government of Somalia in the implementation of the national security plan (De Coning et al. 2014: 11–12).

Following the Elysée Summit for Peace and Security in Africa in December 2013, the AU PSC increased the MISCA strength to 6,000 uniformed personnel in addition to the 152 civilians. By February 2014, sixty-eight police had deployed to MISCA, including four FPUs. Policing duties include, among other aspects, supporting the national authorities to ensure the safety and security of citizens and protecting civilians against imminent threat of physical violence; supporting the security forces and other security agencies in the establishment and maintenance of law and order; supporting capacity-building for the national police and gendarmerie; and supporting security sector reform (SSR) (African Union 2013c).

This multidimensional feature of African peace operations reflects an understanding of the need for integration of military, police and civilian elements to address or at least lay the foundations for unravelling the deep-seated causes of conflict. This trend is likely to continue for the foreseeable future.

Another notable development pertains to increased staffing and function-ality of civilian and police personnel at the continental and regional planning elements (PLANELMs). On the civilian side, staffing levels have increased dramatically in the past five years alone. In 2010, there were approximately seven civilian personnel functioning at the AU and the RECs/RMs – with four at a single regional. By the end of 2014 alone, there were approximately twenty-five civilian planners, including nine at the AU PSOD (comprising a mix of contract and seconded staff), four at the East African Standby Force Coordination Mechanism (EASFCOM), three at the Economic Community of Central African States (ECCAS) and four at the Southern African Development Community (SADC).² At the level of the AU PSOD, the various planners are deeply integrated into and support generally all areas of work as related to the (strategic and operational) planning, deployment and management of missions. Also at the level of the AU PSOD, the increased capacity has meant an increased potential for the elaboration of critical guidance and frameworks that support mandate implementation and mission management, for the development of, for example draft Guidelines for the Protection of Civilians in AU Peace Opera-tions; a draft Administrative Directive for the Recruitment, Deployment and Management of Civilian Personnel in AU Peace and Security Operations; draft Guidelines on Quick Impact Projects (QIPs); and a draft Conduct and Discipline Policy Framework for AU Peace Operations. Regrettably, these still need to move from drafts to agreed and shared policies and guidelines. Additionally, civilian planners are involved in processes leading up to as well as the drafting of mission-critical documents, including, for instance, the Concepts of Opera-tions, Memoranda of Understanding, and so forth. The AU and RECs/RMs have also made impressive strides towards the development of the so-called African Standby Capacity (ASC) Roster, which is intended to support the recruitment, deployment and management of civilian personnel in missions. While these personnel have made noteworthy achievements all round, the extent to which they have been able to be effective has at times been challenged by general capacity, funding and bureaucratic impediments that apply across the AU PSOD.

The picture to date as concerns the police component is less impressive than that presented above on progress with the civilian component. From 2008 onwards, a lot more attention was focused on the development of the police components of the continental and regional PLANELMs to plan, deploy and manage police capacity for field operations. However, a number of critical challenges emerged, largely imposed by the strong initial emphasis on the development of the military elements of the ASF, almost to the exclusion of the police (and civilian) components. For a long time, the police component was subsumed under the military and poorly integrated into the mainstream work on the development of the ASF, with little influence also vis-à-vis decision-making. At the inaugural conference of the AU Police Strategic Support Group

(PSSG) (African Union 2014a)[3] a number of important challenges that impede the effectiveness and visibility of the police component at the AU and the RECs/RMs were identified, including that the AU and the RECs/RMs have achieved varying degrees of development (in terms of organizational structures, capacities, roles and functions) and the absence of strategic guidance and direction on training, operational planning, strategy, policy and doctrine (African Union 2014b: 15–16). All of these challenges (including organization and command structure and roles and responsibilities) will need to be addressed so as to enhance the effectiveness of police planning and management functions at the PLANELMs.

Key areas for improvement

There has without a doubt been some relatively significant progress vis-à-vis the multidimensional imperative of peace operations launched by the AU (and the subregions). This reality is evidenced in the language of mission mandates issued by the PSC and the UN Security Council; the consequent increase in civilian and police personnel in these missions (although not at the strength levels of the military) as well as the diversification of functions they are called upon to undertake; the development of additional frameworks that guide and support mission implementation; and the increased structures and staffing at the level of the PLANELMs to support planning, management and deployment of missions. Notwithstanding these developments, there still remain a number of challenges and opportunities going forward. It is to these that the following section will turn.

Critical functions and capacities

As has already been mentioned by, for example, Dersso (Chapter 3) in this volume, the AU and the RECs/RMs are more often than not deploying into environments that are still characterized by active violence perpetrated by various belligerent and hostile groups, resulting in the suffering, displacement and loss of lives of many. Within this broad context, African operations are required to create a secure environment which will necessitate a substantial presence of military personnel and critical enablers. Working alongside the military, civilian and police personnel will have important roles to play and increasingly so as security conditions improve. The net effort of these African operations is to create the necessary conditions for longer-term post-conflict reconstruction and development efforts, led most likely by the UN.

While the AU may not have the ability to establish and sustain the size and scope of multidimensional missions as compared to the UN, there are critical functions that AU operations should undertake or improve upon so as to ensure better mission implementation and impact and provide an important foundation for a future UN takeover.

Protection of civilians The protection of civilians has become a key area of focus within the broad context of the APSA. Particularly with the establishment of the *AU (Draft) Guidelines for the Protection of Civilians on Peace Support Operations*,[4] there has been increased momentum on this agenda and protection has become a central mandated task in African missions. Even in AMISOM, which was initially not provided with a protection mandate in 2011, the AU PSC has encouraged the incorporation of the draft guidelines into the activities of the mission as well as the development of an AMISOM civilian protection approach (African Union 2011). While missions such as AFISMA and MISCA have been directed to support the respective host country authorities in their primary responsibility to provide protection for their populations, and in this vein to coordinate with other protection actors and strengthen protection in the conduct of their operations and activities, they have struggled to put this into operation. The political commitment to protection by AU member states has often not been matched with an investment in the requisite capacities (staffing) and resources (funding, equipment, etc.) to enable effective implementation. AMISOM, AFISMA and MISCA have all lacked sufficient civilian components to support the mandate to protect civilians under imminent threat.

While the military roles, when it comes to protection, are better understood (albeit there are numerous challenges in this regard which are beyond the scope of this chapter), the role of civilian and police actors requires further clarification and articulation. Mainstreaming protection strategies among the mission components needs additional work, as does the ability of African missions to coordinate on protection with other actors on the ground, be they local authorities or the UN. Given also the robustness or offensive nature of AU operations and the increased likelihood of civilian harm, this internal disconnect within AU operations makes it even more challenging to implement successful risk mitigation strategies that reduce the risks to civilian populations.

Stabilization As Dersso (Chapter 3) has noted in this volume, stabilization in African operations is also becoming a recurrent theme as AU operations are tasked with neutralizing armed conflict while at the same time supporting fledgling efforts at longer-term governance and institution-building. By way of example, AMISOM both supports the Somali Defence Forces (SDF) in the battle against al-Shabaab while also implementing a mandate which directs it to stabilize areas recovered from al-Shabaab, including supporting the extension of the authority of the federal government as well as supporting the capacity of local governments in basic service delivery. Specifically, UN Security Council Resolution 2010 (2011) recognized the critical role police play in the stabilization of Mogadishu and emphasized the importance of AMISOM's police component in supporting the development of an effective Somali police force (Akpasom and Lotze 2014: 18–25). The AU PSC for its part mandated one of its missions for the first time to facilitate and coordinate support by relevant AU institutions and structures for the stabilization and reconstruction of Somalia (African Union 2013d).

AFISMA was also given stabilization responsibilities, including specifically support to Malian authorities in recovering northern territory under the control of extremist elements before transitioning to support for the Malian authorities in maintaining security and consolidating state authority (UNSC 2012). With the transition of authority from AFISMA to the UN Integrated Stabilization Mission in Mali (MINUSMA) on 1 July 2013, the stabilization foundations laid by AFISMA were further elaborated by MINUSMA, which was mandated *inter alia* to stabilize key population centres and support the re-establishment of state authority throughout Mali (United Nations Security Council 2013; Akpasom and Lotze 2014: 21). MISCA too has been tasked with supporting stabilization and the restoration of state authority in the CAR.

Despite the increased attention on stabilization in AU operations, there remains a significant lack of policy guidance or doctrine on stabilization as a concept and how it should be translated in operational terms when it comes to mandate implementation. This aspect will require significant discussion going forward, and there will also be a need to provide training for mission personnel thereon.

The AMISOM civilian component does support stabilization tasks through its various functions, including political and civil affairs, humanitarian liaison and public information. Quick Impact Projects (QIPs) have also been implemented in areas recaptured from al-Shabaab as a means of bringing tangible peace dividends to concerned populations. AMISOM also partakes in stabilization working groups led by the Somali government and provides some operational support to the government in this regard. The configuration of AU operations is still not optimum, however, when it comes to stabilization, and in addition to other important requirements some further civilian and police capacities will have to be invested to support stabilization processes, especially after the conclusion of military operations (ibid.).

Rule of law In given contexts – for example, in the CAR – with significantly deteriorated security conditions lacking rule of law and an ability for national police and justice institutions to stem violence and ensure accountability, the rule of law presents significant needs and challenges for African peace operations personnel, especially the police component. Addressing the gaps requires swift attention not only on the part of these operations but also on that of the broad range of international actors in supporting national authorities in responding to the security challenges and effectively extending their authority in this regard. In Somalia, an important role is being played by AMISOM police (working together with the federal government, the UN and other international partners) to support the establishment of the rule of law in areas that have been secured through military operations.

There are limitations, however, in the implementation of rule-of-law activities for African operations, specifically the inability to support the rule of law beyond policing, to contextualize it within the wider ambit of rule-of-law functions, specifically as they relate to corrections and justice, and to cooperate in this regard with other key actors who supply the considerable resources and expertise necessary for a full elaboration of rule-of-law functions. As recommended by Training for Peace in Africa in its 2014 report on the role of police in AMISOM (De Coning et al. 2014), an ideal solution would be (in addition to the police) the establishment of Rule of Law Units within the mission, comprising civilian judicial experts, corrections officers and others, to support rule-of-law activities. Owing to financial and other constraints, however, the establishment of such units may not be immediately possible and other options should be explored, for instance the secondment of experts through various mechanisms available to the AU[5] or through interested member states. Thus, in terms of improving upon the work of African peace operations in support of the re-establishment of the rule of law in conflict-stricken countries, the AU will need to examine further whether to expand the scope of its rule-of-law engagement and to what degree (relative to the efforts of other actors) and, if it should, what this will entail in practical terms.

Human rights observation A significant degree of attention was generated around the authorization of the deployment of fifty human rights observers for AFISMA (African Union 2013e). The need for the deployment was justified within the context of serious and widespread human rights violations, particularly in the north of Mali, including the recruitment of child soldiers, sexual and other forms of violence against women and children and amputations by extremist groups intent on a strict interpretation of sharia law. The observers were broadly mandated to monitor the human rights situation in the liberated areas and promote and support respect for fundamental human rights and freedoms, and in this way to contribute to the restoration of stability and the promotion of justice in Mali.

The human rights observers were generally well received by the host populations, who saw the observers as much-needed independent eyes on the ground. As one observer stated,

> ... much of our access to the population was due to the fact of our African identify and a belief by locals in our shared values as Africans ... we were seen as an indigenous group ... the UN may see this as mere sentiment but it was an important factor which facilitated our access and acceptability to the local communities we worked amongst. (Akpasom 2014)

AU observers were also able to deploy to areas not accessible to UN observers owing to the organization's more rigid requirements for deployment.

The human rights observer team was beset by a number of challenges that impeded its ability to effectively implement its mandate. For one, there were significant logistical challenges relating to their movement, accommodation, security and medical care that the AU was not able to address adequately. A recurring challenge for AU operations has been that personnel are deployed without fully thinking through or ensuring adequate provisioning for their deployment, and this can have adverse implications for personnel, especially where they are deployed beyond the capital. There was also no distinction made in the specialization of human rights areas and tasks. Thus, all observers were assumed to be knowledgeable in, for example, gender, protection of civilians and even human rights. Additionally, it was also assumed that all observers would approach the tasks of interviewing, evidence collection, monitoring and reporting in the same way, and differences in approach created tensions and/or resulted at times in 'bad practice' in engagement with local communities. Reports from the observers in the various sectors also seemed to vanish into a black hole. These reports were received on an ad hoc basis by the AUC but were never systematically directed in a way in which they could inform further action and decision-making by the relevant political authorities. After the withdrawal of the observers from Mali, there was no post-mission debrief to critically assess implementation in terms of the mandate and to absorb key lessons that could be used to improve implementation in future observation missions.

A final issue worth mentioning is that it is important to keep in mind that the work required to support countries in their transition from conflict to peace and stability is not within the scope of any one single entity to address. But there can be overlap, especially where mandates are similar. AU and UN missions, for example, can within the same operational area be tasked with protection, supporting national dialogue and reconciliation processes, supporting the extension of state authority and promoting and protecting human rights, and so forth. As a result, the comparative strengths and weaknesses of the two organizations will need to be identified, and it will be important to identify practical ways in which coordination and collaboration can be enhanced to ensure an effective and comprehensive response to the crisis at hand.

Improved planning, decision-making and accountability

Although recent peace operation experiences have significantly improved the manner in which the AU conducts planning, there is still scope for further developments in this regard, especially as pertains to the need to achieve integrated planning. One area worth highlighting here that requires additional attention is the conduct of technical assessment mission (TAM) processes. The early planning stages of a mission are usually exclusively conducted by military planners from the PSOD with very little civilian and police representation, whether from the AU PSOD or other relevant departments of the AU Commission (for example, Political Affairs, Human Resources, etc.). TAMs are, however, critical as they provide an opportunity for an assessment of the context and the core needs. This information is then able to feed strategic-level decision-making, mandating and planning processes and can provide a more accurate assessment of resource requirements. When it comes to planning for civilian aspects of missions, an inability to participate in this important process means that, at best, educated guesses or past mission templates are applied in determining core functional areas and structural and staffing configurations. The same applies to the police, which faces the challenge of adequately determining requirements, organization and key mission tasks. Poor assessments translate ultimately into poor or ill-informed decision-making and provisioning as well as a mismatch or misdirection of resources.

It also goes without saying that even if a mission is initially envisaged as being a purely military intervention (for instance, in the context of an ACIRC military operation), it has to be recognized as an instrument of limited duration and purpose. Beyond this there are critical areas that go beyond the scope of the military that will need to be addressed and, as such, right from day one, planning should be conducted in a multidimensional way, considering also when civilian and police functions will need to phase into mission operations. Even at the peak of the military phase of operations, there are still essential civilian and police functions that should be identified and fulfilled.

Another challenge for decision-making pertains to the functioning of the AU Military Staff Committee (MSC), which was established as part of the APSA to provide advice to the PSC on military and security issues for the promotion and maintenance of peace and security on the continent (African Union 2002: Article 13). Given the multidisciplinary requirements in African operations, it is difficult to justify a purely military advisory body for the PSC, which needs to be aware of the full range of issues inherent in the various operations it mandates. Related to this is the poor representation of police chiefs and equivalent civilian representatives in the meetings of the AU Specialized Technical Committee on Defence, Safety and Security (STCDSS), which considers and reflects on matters of defence and security and the work of the AU Commission in this regard. The STCDSS, although dominated by African chiefs of defence staff, also considers and makes/recommends decisions on police and civilian areas of work as undertaken by the AU Commission. Clearly there is a need to revisit the configuration of the STCDSS so that it too becomes more reflective of the multidimensional imperative when it comes to African peace and security.

And finally, accountability is also an important but lacking aspect. When the PSC issues a mandate for an operation, there needs to be better accountability and feedback from the mission on that mandate, especially in terms of the civilian and police elements. The PSC needs to better interrogate and understand not only the achievements that have been made in pursuance of the mandate but also the challenges presented. Was the mandate achievable and did it correspond to the situation and needs on the ground? What were critical points of interface with other key actors on the ground, especially those with seemingly overlapping mandates – what cooperation strategies were utilized and how did these work or not work? Were the resources provided commensurate to the tasks at hand, and if not, how could these be improved in future? What functions can be undertaken that can yield maximum impact; what should be left to other actors and why? How can overall progress on a short-, medium- and long-term basis as against the mandate be evaluated? Unless the AU can develop the necessary feedback loop and accountability mechanisms, decision-making will always inadvertently be conducted in a room that is only partially lit.

Conclusion

The main argument that this chapter has tried to advance is that, contrary to certain views and perceptions on the increased militarization of peace operations on the continent, recent experience has demonstrated an increased complexity in mandated tasks allotted to AU operations, including in areas such as civilian protection, stabilization and the rule of law. Concomitantly, there has been a relative increase in the size and scope of civilian and police roles therein. At the same time, greater momentum has been generated in the establishment of guidance that will inform the work of civilian and police actors in the various missions. The continental and regional PLANELMs are also becoming better configured to enable them to adequately support multi-dimensional mission planning and management processes. The question is no longer about whether or not African operations should be limited to a military response. As is the case elsewhere, multidimensionality in the African context is fast becoming an essential precondition for successful engagement in and support of countries transitioning from conflict to stability. What requires attention is the size and scope of work of the civilian and police elements of African operations, and specifically the identification of critical and/or niche areas of work where African organizations can make the most impact vis-à-vis other actors and partners, including the UN.

Notes

1 Note that in the PSC Protocol, police were included in the reference to 'civilian components', i.e. civilian police. However, with the further development of the ASF, the police were distinguished and developed as a separate component from the civilian component.

2 Civilian staffing at the North African Regional Capability (NARC) was not possible given the suspension of the NARC Secretariat owing to the political crises in that region.

3 Held 23–26 September 2014 in Addis Ababa, Ethiopia. The PSSG was established to enhance coordination, communication, consultation and networking around African policing issues. For further details see African Union (2014b).

4 The guidelines provide guidance on protection for both operational and tactical levels of AU operations.

5 For example, through the 2013 Rapid Secondment Mechanism provided to the AU by the Norwegian government to make civilian experts available rapidly to address emerging peace operation needs.

References

African Union (2002) *Protocol Relating to the Establishment of the Peace and Security Council of the African Union*, Durban: African Union, www.peaceau.org/uploads/psc-protocol-en.pdf, accessed 18 November 2015.

— (2011) *Press Statement of the 279th Meeting of the Peace and Security Council (PSC/PR/BR./[CCLXXIX])*, Press release, Addis Ababa: African Union, http://amisom-au.org/fr/2011/09/press-statement-of-the-279th-meeting-of-the-peace-and-security-council/, accessed 30 November 2015.

— (2013a) *Assembly of the Union, Twenty-First Ordinary Session, 26–27 May 2013, Addis Ababa, Ethiopia. Decisions, Declarations and Resolution*, Addis Ababa: African Union, http:// www.au.int/en/sites/default/files/decisions/9654-assembly_au_dec_474-489_xxi_e.pdf, accessed 18 November 2015.

— (2013b) *Report of the Chairperson of the Commission on the establishment of a Capacity for Immediate Response to Crises (ACIRC) submitted to the 6th ordinary meeting of the Specialised Technical Committee on Defense, Security and Safety (STCDSS)*, 30 April, Addis Ababa: African Union, Unpublished.

— (2013c) *Joint Strategic Concept of Operations for the African-led Support Mission for the Central African Republic*, Unpublished.

— (2013d) *Communiqué of the 356th Meeting of the Peace and Security Council (PSC/BR/COMM (CCCLVI)*, Addis Ababa: African Union, http://www.peaceau.org/en/article/communique-of-the-peace-and-security-council-of-the-african-union-au-at-its-356th-meeting-on-the-strategic-review-of-the-au-mission-in-somalia-amisom, accessed 18 November 2015.

— (2013e) *PSC Communiqué 353rd Meeting at the Level of the Heads of State and Government*, Addis Ababa: African Union, www.peaceau.org/uploads/psc.353.com.mali.25-01-2013-self.pdf, accessed 18 November 2015.

— (2014a) *Report of the Maiden Conference of the African Union Police Strategic Support Group*, Unpublished.

— (2014b) *Terms of Reference for the Police Strategic Support Group*, Addis Ababa: African Union, www.apsta-africa.org/documentation/news/PSSG%20TORs.pdf, accessed 12 February 2015.

Akpasom, Y. (2014) Personal meeting with human rights observer, 8 December, Abuja, Nigeria.

Akpasom, Y. and W. Lotze (2014) 'The shift to stabilization operations: considerations for African peace support operations', *Conflict Trends*, 2: 2–56.

De Coning, C. and Y. Kasumba (2010) *The Civilian Dimension of the African Standby Force*, Durban: African Centre for the Constructive Resolution of Disputes (ACCORD).

De Coning, C., M. Dessu and I. Gjelsvik (2014) *The Role of Police in the African Union Mission in Somalia: Operational Support, Training and Solidarity*, Durban: Training for Peace in Africa, trainingforpeace.org/wp-content/uploads/2014/10/The-Role-of-the-Police-in-AMISOM-TfP-Report-by-de-Coning-Dessu-and-Gjelsvik.pdf, accessed 18 November 2015.

UNSC (United Nations Security Council) (2012) *UNSCR 2085*, New York: United Nations Security Council, www.un.org/en/ga/search/view_doc.asp?symbol=S/RES/2085%282012%29, accessed 18 November 2015.

— (2013) *UNSC Resolution 2100 (2013)*, New York: United Nations Security Council, www.un.org/en/peacekeeping/missions/minusma/documents/mali%20_2100_E_.pdf, accessed 18 November 2015.

9 | Adapting the African Standby Force to a just-in-time readiness model: improved alignment with the emerging African model of peace operations

Cedric de Coning

Introduction

Africa now has a more comprehensive peace and security architecture in place than at any other time since the OAU was founded in 1963. This reflects a high degree of political coherence among African states on the need to improve the peace and security situation on the African continent as a prerequisite for economic development and prosperity. However, many of the structures of the AU still need to become fully operational. Although the APSA has benefited from significant political focus and international support, many aspects of the architecture, including especially those structures responsible for peace operations, still lack institutional capacity, especially the enabling norms, values and policies, and the skilled and experienced human resources, to adequately develop policy and plan and manage peace operations.

Collective norms and values emerge through many generations of challenges and resulting adaptations and refinement. The APSA system has not yet had sufficient opportunity to develop the collective experiences necessary for it to develop into a self-organized peace and security system, with its own culture and shared norms and values. It is still emerging as a new peace and security system, and as such it is still heavily influenced by other global and regional systems, such as the UN, the EU and others. We thus need to understand the current developmental state of peace operations in Africa in the context of the ongoing dynamic evolutionary and adaptive processes that will continue to shape the future direction of African peace operations, and the relationship between African and other – most notably the UN – approaches to peace operations.

In this chapter I reflect back over the past decade to identify the major trends that have shaped the development of African peace operations, and I consider what the implications are for the coming five to ten years, and the direction African peace operations are most likely to take. I argue that there is a need to adapt the ASF current standing readiness model to a just-in-time readiness model, so that the ASF can be better aligned with the new African model of peace operations which is starting to emerge, and I discuss the key characteristics of this model.

The African Standby Force

Over the past decade, the AU, the RECs, such as ECOWAS, ECCAS and SADC, and RMs such as the East Africa Standby Force (EASF) have significantly increased their capacity to undertake and manage peace operations. This is largely due to the decision in 2004 to develop an ASF. This initiative was significant because, for the first time, Africa now had a common position, and a joint action plan, for the development of its peace operations capacity. This meant that the various disparate donor initiatives to enhance Africa's peace operations capacity could be positively channelled to support one coherent effort. The concept is unprecedented. The closest comparison is perhaps the kind of cooperation that has developed around the NATO Partnership for Peace framework.

The African chiefs of defence staff adopted the original Policy Framework of the ASF in May 2003 (African Union 2003). The Framework expands on the provision relating to the ASF in the Peace and Security Council (PSC) Protocol, and it envisages an ASF that is composed of five multidisciplinary (civilian, policy and military) standby forces, made up of national contingents that are based in their home countries. This is not a standing force, therefore, but a network of nationally based units and capacities that are integrated by using a common doctrine, a shared training curriculum, joint exercises and a regional planning element and/or brigade headquarters. These five standby forces (located in north, east, south, west and centre regions) can be used by the AU separately or together, as the need may arise. The type of operations envisaged ranged from observation and monitoring missions to enforcement operations.

In the first phase of the ASF's development, which lasted until 2008, the AU was primarily concerned with putting in place the necessary policy frameworks, including an ASF doctrine, standing operating procedures, a legal framework and a logistics framework. During this period each of the five regions also took steps to establish its standby forces, i.e. they took formal decisions at the subregional level to establish these forces, and they decided on the location for the regional planning element and the composition and organizational structures of the civilian, police and military components of their respective standby forces. In the second phase the regional standby forces were trained and integrated through a series of map, command post and field exercises at regional level, and finally at the continental level, in a command post exercise called 'Exercise Amani' in 2010. The Amani exercise helped the AU to identify which aspects of the ASF it should focus on in the third phase of the development process.

One of the challenges of the ASF is that the AU had to develop its capacity for future peace operations, while at the same time undertaking current operations. In July 2011, these two parallel streams met for the first time when the AU and the EASF signed an agreement whereby that region's standby force deployed staff officers to the headquarters of the AU Mission in Somalia (AMISOM).

Although considerable progress has been achieved since the ASF Framework was first approved in 2003, the operationalization of the ASF has been slower than anticipated, and has been predominantly focused on the military aspects of peace operations. As Yvonne Akpasom (Chapter 8) argues in this book, one of the key remaining challenges is the need to equally develop the civilian and police dimensions of the ASF Framework so that the multidimensional nature of contemporary peace operations can be fully integrated into the African peace operations concept. Several initiatives are under way to address the development of the police and civilian dimension of the ASF and steady progress is being made in this regard (De Coning and Kasumba 2010).

However, the ASF is likely to continue to suffer from a culture of perpetual uncertainty until it is actually used to mobilize an African or regional peace operation. This is because the ASF policies and procedures remain, in a sense, theoretical until an opportunity has arisen where they can be tested. Several aspects remain unclear, and will probably only be resolved when the need arises to mobilize the ASF in a specific mission context. Although its function as a tool to prepare and mobilize peacekeepers for an operation is yet to be utilized fully, it has already yielded benefits in that it serves as a vehicle for integrating a common African approach to peace operations. It has provided a platform for the development of common doctrine, common training and for regional and continental exercises, and this has contributed to developing a common African understanding and approach to peace operations. At this point in time only NATO, the EU and Africa have reached this level of regional integration.

The African Capacity for Immediate Response to Crises

Over the last decade, in a parallel development to the establishment of the ASF, the AU has deployed several peace operations, including to Burundi (AMIB), the CAR, Darfur (AMIS), Mali (AFISMA) and Somalia (AMISOM). Over time, frustration built up around the tension between the investment in an ASF capability that would be ready only in 2010, later postponed to 2015, and the need to find and deploy troops, police officers and civilians, as well as their equipment, to new and ongoing operations. This tension came to a head in 2012 when the government of Mali asked France to intervene in its crisis because the AU and ECOWAS were perceived to be unable to deploy their forces rapidly enough to deal decisively with the unfolding crisis there (Théroux-Bénoni 2013).

As a result of this frustration, a number of African countries decided to jointly create the ACIRC in January 2013. The ACIRC was presented as an interim measure, aimed at addressing the rapid response deficit until such time as the ASF and its RDC reached full operational capability. The ACIRC is a voluntary arrangement whereby those countries with the necessary capabilities make them available under the auspices of the AU. The distinguishing feature of the ACIRC is that it proposes a coalition of the willing with deployment, initially at the contributors' own cost, under a lead-nation model. However, such a coalition will require AU approval for it to operate under AU auspices. See Jide Okeke's (Chapter 7) and Solomon Dersso's (Chapter 3) chapters in this book for a more detailed explanation of the ACIRC.

These factors – voluntary participation, coalition of the willing, lead nation, self-funded – were all part of the design of the ACIRC because they are assumed to contribute to rapid deployment. However, my assessment is that because the ACIRC model is voluntary, it will also fail to address the AU's need for a predictable rapid deployment capability. In practice 'voluntary' means that countries will be willing to deploy at their own cost only when they have dire national interests at stake (Comfort 2013).

2013 assessment of the ASF

In the context of the Mali experience and the decision to establish the ACIRC, the January 2013 AU General Assembly also asked for an assessment of the progress made to date with the establishment of the ASF. To meet this request, the chairperson of the Commission appointed an Independent Panel of Experts in July 2013 to conduct a comprehensive assessment of the ASF.[1] The Panel submitted their report in December 2013, and in January 2014 the report and the recommendations of the Panel were endorsed by both the ministers of defence and security and the AU Summit (African Union 2013).

The Panel found that despite progress towards operationalizing the ASF, significant shortcomings, gaps and obstacles still remain. The Panel was of the opinion that at the current pace and scope of effort, it is unlikely that the ASF will achieve full operational capability by the end of 2015. Therefore, the Panel recommended that in order to achieve full operational capability by the end of 2015, a major effort would be needed. The Panel presented a plan of action that was aimed at addressing those key areas that, if left unaddressed, would make it impossible to achieve full operational capability.

The Panel also recommended that the AU give special attention to the financing of its peace operations. The Panel found that the most significant constraint on African peace operations, and the ability to respond rapidly to unfolding crises, is the inability of the AU member states to fund their own operations. The AU cannot make its own independent decisions regarding the mandate, scope, size and duration of its peace operations as long as it is dependent on external partners to cover the cost of these operations. The Panel thus strongly supported the emphasis the AU is currently placing on generating its own resources. At the same time, the Panel recommended that the AU take steps to reduce the cost of the ASF by right-sizing its concept, structures and policies, including especially the mission support concept.

The Panel also recommended that the AU consider undertaking a high-level strategic review of the future of the ASF and African peace support operations. The ASF was designed on assumptions derived mainly from the UN's multidimensional peacekeeping experiences of the 1990s. Since then, the AU, the RECs/RMs and other AU coordinated coalitions of the willing have managed peace operations of their own in Burundi, against Boko Haram, in the CAR, in Comoros, in Darfur, against the Lord's Resistance Army, in Mali and in Somalia. As a result of these operational experiences, the AU, the regions and the member states involved have started to develop their own body of knowledge on African-led peace operations. A significant gap has opened up between the consensual peacekeeping model the ASF is designed for, and the actual peace enforcement and stabilization operations the AU has been called on to undertake in Somalia, Mali and the CAR. The Panel argued that the existing ASF Policy Framework should be reviewed against these experiences and be aligned with the realities of the African peace operation experience. This will ensure that a new strategic vision for African peace operations and the ASF will be in place that can inform the future of the ASF beyond 2015. Although this recommendation, together with the rest of the report, was endorsed by the AU heads of state, the AU Commission has not, to date, taken any steps to appoint such a high-level panel. However, in 2015 the AU cooperated closely with an independent high-level panel appointed by the UN secretary general in 2014 to undertake a review of UN peace operations. Furthermore, on 30 April 2015, the AU Peace and Security Council adopted an African Common Position on UN Peace Operations that does give the AU strategic direction for its relationship with UN peace operations.

We cannot reflect on the standby capacity of the ASF without taking into account the significant increase in actual African peace operations capacity since the launch of the ASF project a decade ago (De Coning 2014). This increase is reflected in the number and scale of peace operations undertaken by the AU over this period, and the contributions from African TCCs to UN peacekeeping operations. In total, approximately 40,000 uniformed and civilian personnel were mandated to serve in African peace operations in 2013 (approximately 71,000 if the joint AU–UN hybrid mission in Darfur is taken into account as well).[2] In addition, African contributions to UN peacekeeping operations have increased steadily during this period – from a little over 10,000 per annum in 2003, when the ASF project was launched, to approximately 35,000 per annum by 2013. This means that in 2013 more than 75,000 African peacekeepers served in African and UN peace operations. Today Africans make up the largest proportion of the UN's civilian, police and military peace operation staff. As of March 2015, approximately 60 per cent of the UN's 5,200 international civilian peace operations staff and about 80 per cent of its 11,600 local staff are African. In addition, Africa has now become the largest regional contributor of police and soldiers to UN peace operations, and contributes approximately 48 per cent of the UN's 106,000 uniformed peacekeepers. Six of the top ten UN TCCs are from Africa, with Ethiopia now the largest contributor to peace operations in the world if one takes both their UN (approximately 7,700) and AU (approximately 4,050) contributions into account.[3]

Since the establishment of the ASF, African peace operations have been deployed to Burundi, against Boko Haram, to the CAR, to Comoros, to Darfur, against the Lord's Resistance Army, to Mali and to Somalia (see Table 1.1). Each of these missions involved political decision-making processes, planning, deployment, strategic and operational management and mission support. Several of these missions were also handed over to the UN and liquidated. Together they represent a significant demonstration of African capacity and experience. All these missions have been undertaken with support from the UN, EU and bilateral partners, and they thus also reflect a growing body of experience with various forms of partnerships and collaborative action. In most of these missions the ASF planning elements at the continental and regional levels have been involved in the planning and management of the missions, and the ASF regional centres of excellence have been involved in the training, preparation and evaluation of these missions.

As Solomon Dersso and Jide Okeke explain in their chapters in this book, the most recent operation against Boko Haram is a case in point. The countries in the Lake Chad Basin decided to activate their MNJTF mechanism and to take coordinated action against Boko Haram. However, to link the MNJTF coalition with the formal structures of the AU and UN, so that it could obtain the necessary political authority and financial and logistical support, the AU used the ASF planning element capacities in ECCAS and ECOWAS to establish a regional forward headquarters that could support the MNJTF force headquarters, and act as a link to the AU in Addis, which acted as the strategic headquarters for the mission. This example illustrates how ASF capacities are already being used to support new and ongoing missions.

Despite this record, some observers continue to claim that the ASF is ineffective because its standing readiness model has not yet been utilized as envisaged in the original policy framework, i.e. the ASF has not yet deployed one of its regional rapid deployment battle groups or its standby brigades. The Panel argued that this distinction between the ASF, understood as the units, equipment and personnel pledged under the ASF, and the actual units and personnel deployed to African peace operations is somewhat artificial. The 75,000 African peacekeepers deployed in 2013 come from the same member states that have pledged contributions to the ASF, which demonstrates that these member states do have these capabilities and are able to deploy them when needed. The capacity thus exists at member-state level, and has been used in a range of African and UN operations, as the numbers quoted earlier reflect. It is just that the AU and the RECs have not yet opted to activate the actual ASF standby mechanisms. I will reflect on why this has been the case in the next section.

When it comes to rapid deployment, however, it should be noted that the AU, together with its TCCs and partners, has deployed forces into Somalia and the CAR far more rapidly than the EU or the UN. The Panel therefore argued that Africa's actual deployed capacity and its actual rapid deployment record are stronger indicators of Africa's real peace operation capability than the pledges reflected in the ASF. At the same time, we need to acknowledge that the ASF is not only going to generate value at some point in the future; it is already significantly contributing to preparing the capabilities that are deployed to actual African and UN peace operations. For this reason, the Panel recommends that, as of 2016, all AU operations should be deployed as ASF operations.

Challenges related to the standby readiness model

When political or social tensions result in violent conflict, the solution that is usually most prominently on the table is the rapid deployment of a peace support operation, as in the cases of the CAR and South Sudan. This is why the 2002 Protocol establishing the African Union's Peace and Security Council (PSC) provided for the establishment of an ASF. When fully operational, the RDC of the ASF should be on standing readiness to deploy within fourteen days in response to mass-atrocity crimes.

This target has, however, proved to be quite a challenge. In fact, there is no international or regional organization that can deploy such a force within fourteen days. There are only a handful of countries in the world that have the kind of standing readiness capacity to deploy at such speeds. If pursuing this kind of response time is unrealistic, is it not time to take stock and question whether this is the type of model that we should continue to invest our effort in?

I argue that it is time for the ASF to shift from a standing readiness model to a just-in-time rapid response model. I argue that the actual experience of the AU differs significantly enough from the ASF model to warrant a substantial adjustment in the ASF, so that the policy can catch up with the reality.

Africa has the capacity to deploy rapidly, with the support of its international partners, but this capacity resides at national, not regional, level. The stabilization missions that the AU has been called on to undertake require TCCs and PCCs that have a strategic interest in the outcome. This means that each conflict will have its own unique set of interested parties. Thus, no preformed standby agreement will meet the unique and context-specific needs of the case at hand. What has happened in each case – Burundi, Boko Haram, the CAR, Comoros, Darfur, Lord's Resistance Army, Mali and Somalia – is that a unique coalition of the willing came together to form a mission, and I include here the TCCs, PCCs and their international partners. This is why it is necessary to adapt the ASF to a just-in-time model.

The logic behind the standby concept is that the ability to rapidly deploy a peace operation will be greatly enhanced if you pre-select soldiers, police officers and civilian experts; prepare and train them; make sure they have the necessary equipment and support systems in place; and then place them on a standing readiness mode, waiting for a decision to deploy them. The standby model assumes that such a standing readiness capacity is a necessary precondition for rapid deployment, but acknowledges that it is not sufficient to ensure that a peace operation can be rapidly deployed when faced with a dire crisis. Two additional factors have been highlighted in the 2013 ASF Assessment, namely the political decision-making process and the financing of peace operations.

The ASF and all other such standby arrangements suffer from two further interrelated vulnerabilities. The first is the political will of the contributing countries to participate in any given operation. Agreeing to participate in a standby arrangement is one thing, but agreeing to participate in a specific peace operation is a separate decision altogether. The second requires a match between the context-specific needs of a specific mission at hand and the off-the-shelf generic design of the standby force. It is a combination of these two vulnerabilities that has undermined all international efforts to date to establish standby arrangements that can generate predictable rapid response mechanisms (De Coning 2014).

There are no international examples where the preformed standby brigade concept has been used successfully to date. The UN Standby High-Readiness Brigade (SHIRBRIG) initiative, the EU Battle Group concept and the ASF share these same vulnerabilities (Koops and Varwick 2008). The SHIRBRIG initiative has already been abandoned, and it is unlikely that the EU Battle Group and the ASF's standing readiness capacity will be used as envisaged. This is because each crisis is unique and it is unlikely that a generic standby capacity can sufficiently match the needs, in terms of both the political coalition and the operational capabilities, posed by the specific challenge.

Each crisis requires a context-specific solution, including the coming together of a unique set of countries that have a political interest in the resolution of the conflict, or have an interest in being part of that particular mission. Each crisis also requires a slightly different set of capacities, and the off-the-shelf generic standby brigade model does not meet such needs. This explains why the AU, the EU and the UN have not found a direct use for their standing readiness arrangements to date.

Rapid deployment can, of course, happen only if there are capabilities at national level that can be deployed. The basic assumption or logic of the standby model thus holds true at national level, but falls apart when it is applied at the multinational level. This is because at this level the decisive factor is not capabilities and readiness, but how those capabilities are coalesced in a political coalition that forges together political will, financial means, the capacity to plan, deploy and manage an operation and the national capabilities that can be deployed.

National interest is a subtle and often indirect driver in the consensual-type of peace operations the UN and EU typically undertake, but it is still vitally important to mobilize political will to contribute troops. In the AU context, where the operations undertaken to date have almost all been peace enforcement operations with a stabilization mandate that requires a higher degree of intensity, robustness and exposure to risk, the national interest of especially the major troop-contributing countries has been of decisive importance. The missions in both Somalia and the CAR have sustained heavy losses (Leijenaar and Helmoed 2014). A country with no interest in a given crisis is unlikely to agree to its capabilities being deployed in a high-intensity and high-risk operation, just because they agreed to be part of a regional standby arrangement. This goes a long way to explaining why the ASF, and its RDC, have not yet been utilized in the way envisaged. At the same time, many of the countries that participate in the East African Standby Force arrangement are deployed and operating together in AMISOM. Likewise, many of the countries that are members of ECCAS have contributed troops to MISCA. The critical issue here is the assumption that all the countries that have agreed to participate in the ASF will be willing to deploy together via the ASF, regardless of the mission. This is why I have pointed out the difference between participating in the ASF project for the sake of regional and continental cooperation and integration, and actual deployments that are driven by interests, especially when it comes to stabilization operations that are likely to require the use of offensive doctrines.

What we can thus conclude from the ASF experience to date is that the general effort to establish the ASF has contributed significantly to the capacity of the AU, the regions and AU member states to plan, prepare, train and deploy military, police and civilian capacities to actual missions. However, the standing readiness dimension of the ASF concept – that is, the idea of specific pre-identified military and police units being prepared, verified and then placed on standing readiness, so that they can be deployed rapidly when called upon to do so – has not been used, and is unlikely to be used, as assumed in the design of the ASF.

This leads to the recommendation that the post-2015 ASF concept should be adjusted to one that is aimed at generating a just-in-time capacity, rather than a standing readiness capacity. A just-in-time model will focus on developing common standards and procedures, including through joint training and exercises. It should also have a special focus on developing AU, regional and national planning, command, mission management and mission support capabilities.

There may be a place for the ACIRC lead-nation model, especially in dire emergencies when rapid response is critical, but the just-in-time ASF model proposed here foresees situations where the AU, in close cooperation with the regions, plays the lead role in putting together, planning, deploying and commanding its own peace operations.

This proposal does not imply that we should abandon the ASF, only that we move away from the standing readiness model, and in its place develop a just-in-time model. At the national level many AU member states should, and do, have some units on standby to respond to national and international crises regardless of the ASF, so the suggestion is not that member states move away from the standing readiness concept at national level.

A just-in-time model will require a leaner ASF investment, because less effort will be needed to manage the pledging and verification of specific units, and to manage the model of rotating the responsibility for being on standing readiness among regions. This shift will allow the AU and the regions to focus more on the preparation of just-in-time modalities and the planning for and management of actual missions. This would be a much more realistic use of limited resources.

The one exception is the civilian dimension of the ASF. As Yvonne Akpasom points out in this book, nations have military and police capacities that they can make available for African peace operations, but they do not deploy civilian experts in the same way. Civilian experts are hired by the AU in their individual capacities. This is why it is necessary for the AU, in cooperation with the regions and the member states, to continue to identify, train and roster civilian experts in political affairs, human rights, public information, humanitarian liaison, and all the other specialities identified in the ASF Civilian Policy Framework (De Coning and Kasumba 2010).

It is now time, based on our experience with the ASF and actual AU operations over the past decade, to take stock and acknowledge that the standing readiness aspect of the ASF concept is not going to generate the kind of predictable rapid response the AU member states desired when they agreed to establish the ASF. Instead we should shift our focus to a just-in-time model based on three elements:

1. the modalities necessary to put together context-specific coalitions consisting of the AU, regions, member states and partners;
2. the ability of member states to contribute military, police and civilian capabilities; and
3. the ability of the AU and regions to plan, deploy, manage and support peace operations.

Mali may have been a reminder that rapid deployment will not always be possible, but Somalia and the CAR have also shown us that the AU, together with its member states and partners, can deploy troops at remarkable speed. The reasons why the AU was able to deploy much faster in the latter cases have less to do with pre-designed standing readiness arrangements and more to do with the kind of political will the AU was able to generate, and the context-specific coalitions the AU, interested member states and partners were able to put together. This is why a just-in-time standby arrangement is likely to be the more realistic and cost-effective option for the future of the ASF.

Implications for the AU–UN relationship

The most important regional relationship for the UN is its relationship with the AU (UN 2015). As pointed out earlier, African capacities are an important resource for UN peacekeeping, currently contributing approximately 45 per cent of the UN's uniformed personnel, 60 per cent of its international civilian personnel and 80 per cent of its local staff. At the same time, UN support is a critical enabler for AU operations, and the UN is an important exit strategy partner for the AU. The effectiveness of both the UN and the AU thus hinges on mutually interdependence on several levels. The UN will have to consider more predictable ways in which the UN and other partners can support the AU and regional peace operations, such as the MNJTF operations against Boko Haram.

At the strategic level the UN and the AU should foster a common narrative that is mutually reinforcing and respectful of the other's roles. At the operational level the UN and AU can develop joint guidelines on transitions. Such an agreed joint approach can make it easier for both organizations to involve each other from the earliest stages in assessments, planning, coordination mechanisms, mission support, benchmarks and evaluation.

More efforts are needed to creatively and innovatively find ways to support African peace operations. For instance, the UN can make some of its Department of Field Service capabilities available to the AU, including its Brindisi and Kampala logistical depots; include the AU in some on-call procurement arrangements, for instance strategic airlift; and partner with the AU in developing essential mission support planning and managing capabilities in the AU Commission and AU missions.

African peace operations represent local responses to global problems. Most African conflicts are global in the sense that they are heavily influenced, if not driven, by external factors such as the global war on terror; the exploitation of natural resources by multinationals; capital flight facilitated and solicited by the international banking system; and transnational organized crime, driven by markets in the West for narcotics, human trafficking, timber and illegally caught fish. Effective African peace operations thus represent a significant contribution to the global common good.

A partnership model has emerged whereby the AU and regional entities, with support from the UN and partners, acted as first responders to African crises in, for instance, Burundi, the CAR, Darfur and Mali. When basic stability was achieved, these missions were handed over to the UN, and the African military and police peacekeepers were re-hatted and became UN peacekeepers (De Coning, Gelot and Karlsrud 2015). Somalia has been the exception in that sufficient stability has not yet been achieved to trigger a handover to the UN. However, the AU and UN are jointly developing benchmarks for a future transition. In the meantime, AMISOM and the United Nations Assistance Mission in Somalia (UNSOM) are working closely together and both are supported by UNSOA.

The AU lacks predictable funding for its peace operations, and this dilemma impacts negatively on the UN. The UN had to – as a last resort – take over the AU's missions in Mali and the CAR earlier than it would have had to if the AU missions had had sufficient resources. As a result, the UN had to deploy stabilization-type missions that forced it to go beyond its peacekeeping principles and doctrine. The decision by the January 2015 AU Summit that the AU should contribute at least 25 per cent of the cost of AU-led peace operations will, if implemented, contribute significantly to addressing the funding dilemma. In addition to the direct injection of resources, the decision signals African resolve and political will, and this is likely to also encourage the AU's partners to support AU operations. The recommendation of the UN High-level Independent Panel on Peace Operations that it is in the UN's interest to help the AU to find more predictable and sustainable sources of funding for AU-led peace operations, including considering funding for AU operations from UN assessed contributions, gives further momentum to this new drive behind finding a solution to the funding dilemma.

Conclusion

Over the past decade, the AU and regional organizations have significantly increased their capacity to undertake and manage peace operations. In the process an African model of peace operations has started to emerge. This model is characterized by the stabilization nature of African peace operations, which differs in significant ways from UN peacekeeping doctrine. A further characteristic is that African peace operations are typically short, intense operations that hand over to the UN peacekeeping operations once sufficient stability has been restored. Lastly, these operations are partnership operations that are dependent on partners for both financial and logistical sustainment, as well as strategic political alignment.

Stabilization operations are not military solutions; they can at best generate temporary stability so that a political context can be shaped that is conducive to finding political solutions to the problem. However, as the AU, the UN, the EU, the RECs and others all contribute mere facets of the overall effort, issues of strategic coherence take on a new importance.

I have argued that it is time for the ASF to shift from a standing readiness model to a just-in-time readiness model. I have argued that each conflict is unique and thus requires an exclusive response, including a distinctive set of actors, both African and international, pulled together in a coalition of the willing because they each have a particular interest in addressing the conflict in question. It is very rare that an off-the-shelf or pre-designed standby model will be able to meet the specific requirements of a given challenge. In fact, there is no international example today of a successful standby model. As a result, the ASF has not yet deployed its brigades or RDC battle groups, and I argue that it is unlikely that they will ever be deployed in that format.

However, the same countries that have pledged civilians, police officers and troops to the ASF have deployed over 75,000 peacekeepers to UN and AU operations. Thus, the capacity exists and is being utilized, but not via the ASF's standing readiness mechanism. I argue that this is because the ASF mechanism, as currently designed, is unable to meet the need for context-specific solutions, and therefore the ASF should change from a standing readiness model to a just-in-time readiness model so that it can be better aligned with the emerging model of African peace operations.

One of the most significant developments in the African context is the informal division of roles that has emerged around the sequencing of peace operations. The pattern that is taking shape is that the AU, or one of the RECs, first deploys a stabilization operation, which is then followed by a UN peacekeeping operation, once basic stability has been restored. This informal division of roles has given both the AU and the UN the opportunity to develop a more strategic partnership that can both serve this current division of work and track and adapt to future evolutions in the UN and AU relationship.

In describing the African model of peace operations I do not mean to suggest that the AU has consolidated, or should consolidate, its capacities around this one model. The model has evolved out of the African experiences of the last decade and will continue to evolve. The AU is responding to a highly dynamic and fast-changing environment, and its peace and security tools will need to be highly flexible to plug-and-play with a wide range of scenarios. For instance, the operations in the Lake Chad Basin are very different in nature from AU operations in Somalia and the CAR, and the AU and RECs/RMs need to remain nimble in order to absorb the unique bottom-up manifestations of such coalitions of the willing. At the same time there are similarities and lessons that can be shared, and the AU can thus play an important role by being the strategic point of convergence for policy, doctrine, best practices and mission planning, management and evaluation.

Notes

1 The author was a member of the Panel but writes here in his personal capacity.

2 All deployment figures in this chapter are based on either the UN *Peacekeeping Fact Sheet*, available at www.un.org/en/peacekeeping/resources/statistics/factsheet.shtml, accessed on 8 May 2014, or calculated based on Lotze (2014).

3 In comparison, the South-East Asian countries together contribute approximately 30 per cent of the UN's uniformed peacekeepers.

References

African Union (2003) *Policy Framework for the Establishment of the African Standby Force and the Military Staff Committee*, Addis Ababa: African Union, http://www.peaceau.org/uploads/asf-policy-framework-en.pdf, accessed 18 November 2015.

— (2013) *Report of the Independent Panel of Experts, Assessment of the African Standby Force and Plan of Action for achieving full operational capability by 2015*, Addis Ababa: African Union, Unpublished.

Comfort, E. (2013) 'The problems with African solutions', Blog, 2 December, http://blog.crisisgroup.org/africa/2013/12/02/the-problems-with-african-solutions/, accessed 18 November 2015.

De Coning, C. (2014) 'Enhancing the efficiency of the ASF: the case for a shift to a just-in-time rapid response model', *Conflict Trends*, 2: 34–40.

De Coning, C. and Y. Kasumba (2010) *The Civilian Dimension of the African Standby Force*, Durban: African Centre for the Constructive Resolution of Disputes (ACCORD).

De Coning, C., L. Gelot and J. Karlsrud (2015) *Strategic Options for the Future of African Peace Operations: 2015–2025*, Oslo/Uppsala: Norwegian Institute of International Affairs/Nordic Africa Institute.

Koops, J. and J. Varwick (2008) *Ten Years of SHIRBRIG: Lessons Learned, Development Prospects and Strategic Opportunities for Germany*, Berlin: Global Public Policy Institute, http://mercury.ethz.ch/serviceengine/Files/ISN/87403/ipublicationdocument_singledocument/b69a4818-0903-4056-b8a8-ef9863b98afe/en/No_11_Ten_Years_of_Shirbrig.pdf, accessed 18 November 2015.

Leijenaar, A. and H. Heitman (2014) *Africa Can Solve Its Own Problems with Proper Planning and Full Implementation of the African Standby Force*, Pretoria: Institute of Security Studies, https://www.issafrica.org/iss-today/africa-can-solve-its-own-problems-with-proper-planning-and-full-implementation-of-the-african-standby-force, accessed 18 November 2015.

Lotze, W. (2014) 'Strengthening African peace support operations: nine lessons for the African Standby Force', ZIF Policy Briefing, www.zif-berlin.org/fileadmin/uploads/analyse/dokumente/veroeffentlichungen/ZIF_Policy_Briefing_Walter_Lotze_Dec_2013.pdf, accessed 18 November 2015.

Théroux-Bénoni, L. A. (2013) *Mali in the aftermath of the French military intervention: new opportunities or back to square one?*, Dakar: Institute for Security Studies, https://www.issafrica.org/publications/situation-reports/mali-in-the-aftermath-of-the-french-military-intervention-le-mali-au-lendemain-de-de-loperation-militaire-francaise, accessed 18 November 2015. ·

UN (United Nations) (2015) *Report of the High-level Independent Panel on United Nations Peace Operations: Uniting our Strengths for Peace – Politics, Partnership and People*, 16 June, New York: United Nations, www.un.org/sg/pdf/HIPPO_Report_1_June_2015.pdf, accessed 18 November 2015.

10 | African peace operations: trends and future scenarios, conclusions and recommendations

Cedric de Coning, Linnéa Gelot and John Karlsrud

The AU and the RECs/RMs have had to respond to increasingly complex security environments over the last decade, and the emergent African model of peace operations is now at odds with the mission scenarios and assumptions that underpinned the original ASF framework. There is a need for regular discussions among strategic partners on common norms, goals and needs. Further, it is important to promote interdepartmental coordination and the adoption of common objectives to avoid stovepiping and duplication of efforts. Following up on Darkwa's (Chapter 5) recommendation of better articulation of the needs of the continent in a cohesive strategy, we call for more inter-departmental and inter-institutional joint conflict analyses, to enable shared understanding of root causes, on triggering factors and on conflict prevention and mediation strategies. The RECs, with their in-depth subregional and local knowledge, could provide a platform for partners to perform these analyses.

With the ASF due to achieve full operational capability (FOC) by the end of 2015, the question now is how the ASF will be utilized in the future, and more generally what the future holds for the ASF and African peace operations beyond 2015. The independent panel of experts appointed by the chairperson of the AU Commission in 2013 to review the progress made by the ASF recommended that the existing ASF Policy Framework should be reviewed, and be aligned with the realities of the African peace operation experience. In this regard, the AU would benefit from a high-level strategic review of African peace operations, similar to the one that UN Secretary General Ban Ki-moon appointed in 2014 to review UN peace operations. Such an under-taking could enable the AU to prepare for the next decade on the basis of a shared strategic vision for ASF operations that is relevant to the current and near-future context, and adjusted to the strategic objectives of the AU's *Agenda 2063* and *Silencing the Guns*.

Strategic partnerships

An important aspect of African peace operations beyond 2015 will be the continuous development of the partnerships between African actors and the

UN, the EU and other actors with vested interests in Africa's stability and development. The past decade has brought new and creative forms of cooperation and many of these ad hoc collaborations are worth institutionalizing further. Partners of African institutions are undergoing change in this direction. The EU and the European External Action Service (EEAS) are moving towards an increasingly structured strategic partnership with Africa on peace and security (Peen-Rodt and Okeke 2013). In 2014, NATO and the AU agreed to formalize their relations and NATO established a liaison office at the AU headquarters. The AU and China are also exploring increased peace and security cooperation, including Chinese support for AU-led peace operations. In September 2015, China's permanent observer to the AU contributed a further US$1.2 million to the AU towards the cost of running AMISOM (African Union 2015).Other individual states, such as Japan, Russia, Turkey and India, have also moved in the direction of establishing strategic partnerships with the AU/APSA and with African states.

The UN has experienced a rise in the number of operations during a period of financial austerity, with increasing deployments to situations that stretch the understanding of what situations UN peacekeeping is intended to cover (Karlsrud 2015). The UN thus understands the value of the AU assuming a greater role in stabilization – a role that the AU itself wants to play – and there is a shared need to improve cooperation between the AU and the UN – for instance, when it comes to improving the modalities for managing transitions from AU to UN operations. As the UN High-level Independent Panel on Peace Operations observed, strategic partnerships, including between the UN and regional organizations, will be a central characteristic of peace operations over the coming decade. It is now a firmly established pattern that no conflict can be comprehensively addressed by the AU, the UN or any other actor alone. Each conflict will see the presence of a number of actors such as the UN, the AU, the EU and the relevant REC or RM. A number of states may be particularly engaged, both African and international, along with a range of development and humanitarian actors. UN Secretary General Ban Ki-moon endorsed the report of the High-level Independent Panel on UN Peace Operations in September 2015. Moreover, in 2015 the UN undertook a review of its peacebuilding architecture, a review of progress made with the implementation of UNSC Resolution 1325 on Women, Peace and Security, as well as establishing new goals for global sustainable development following the expiry of the Millennium Development Goals. These global policy-making processes highlighted the contemporary challenges to which UN and African peacekeepers have to respond.

Still-remaining areas of tension in the AU–UN partnership include differing ideas on the preconditions for deployment and transitions (as the AU is often called upon to deploy in active conflicts, where there is no viable ceasefire and/or peace agreement); differing interpretations of norms such as 'protection of civilians' or 'unconstitutional' changes of government; differing conceptualizations of and approaches to the use of force and combat roles in peace operations; challenges and conflicts surrounding the principle of subsidiarity; and proposals and expectations for financing African peace operations.

Two types of partnership will be key. The first, further developing African capacity and further increasing the African voice on the international stage, will be linked to the use of the phrase 'strategic partnership'. Strategic partnership is about the wish to clarify on all sides the shared long-term political objectives between African and non-African institutions and to regularize or institutionalize mechanisms in support of those objectives. The second is related to operational coherence and is aimed at ensuring that the large number of actors mentioned above, who are always likely to be engaged in one form or other in any peace operations context, engage in a manner that is coordinated among the external actors and aligned with the actions of national authorities and local actors. The term 'strategic coherence' can be used to reflect the need for all the actors to have a common understanding of the objectives they are pursuing in a particular case, and the role that each actor is playing to contribute towards the larger strategic objectives.

At the same time, reflection will be needed on how partnerships and peace operations fit into the larger 'Africa rising' narrative, i.e. in a context where conflict is no longer at the core of Africa's identity, but associated merely with a few countries on the continent that are not able to stabilize, develop and consolidate at the same pace as the rest. Consultations among strategic partners should consider shared political objectives in a broader light, beyond urgent peacemaking priorities.

Operationalizing the ASF, the RDC and harmonizing with the ACIRC

Seeing that the actual experience of the AU over the last decade has differed significantly from what was envisaged under the ASF framework, it is time to adjust the ASF model so that the capacities being developed can better reflect the kinds of missions the AU is likely to undertake. There is a need to consider what specialized and niche capacities and capabilities the AU and the RECs/RMs need to develop or enhance, so as to ensure they are prepared for the kinds of operation they are likely to be called on to undertake over the next decade. These capacities could include various mobility-enhancing capabilities such as helicopters and planes, combat logistics, information-gathering capabilities, specialized and formed police units, troop protection capabilities and political functions. How can the AU achieve the right balance between necessary capacities/capabilities and resource constraints?

Efforts are now under way to harmonize the ASF and the ACIRC initiatives through the AMANI exercise cycle and the implementation of the revised

ASF–ACIRC Roadmap. As Okeke (Chapter 7) and Dersso (Chapter 3) have highlighted, the most pressing question is not whether to go with either the ASF or the ACIRC, but how to further develop the RDC of the ASF and harmonize it with the ACIRC. However, despite the decision by the AU Assembly in 2014 to ensure harmonization of the ASF and the ACIRC, both processes seem to have proceeded in parallel, or at best through selective attempts to harmonize the two mechanisms.

The ASF is likely to remain the main framework for African peace operations. As de Coning (Chapter 9) has argued in this book, even if the ASF is not be deployed in the standby brigade format envisaged in the original framework, it will continue to be of significant value for future operations as a repository of doctrine, standards and training guidelines, by providing a common understanding of an African approach to peace operations.

Drawing on experience, there should be further reflection on the various scenarios most likely for the deployment of African peace operations. Experiences from these operations should also feed into the future development of the ASF. Moreover, the regional and local legitimacy of interventions is a central point, and one that requires collective responses on the continent. As de Coning (Chapter 9) has pointed out, actual deployed capability to date testifies to the African political commitment, even beyond the ambitions set out in the ASF concept. However, this commitment is not clearly in line with the 'collective security' assumption underpinning the standby brigades as originally conceived, since African states respond to conflicts more on a coalition-of-the-willing basis. Therefore, continued reflection is needed on how the AU might ensure political oversight and lines of accountability.

Ensuring UN, AU and where relevant REC/RM authorization is important for political, legal and legitimacy reasons. However, all AU operations to date have taken place on invitation from or with the consent of the host state. Individual states or coalitions with high stakes involved may occasionally choose to act rapidly, as was the case in the Lake Chad Basin to counter Boko Haram. In these cases the AU PSC, and the UNSC, are likely to endorse these missions soon after they have deployed. Thus, a lead-nation concept seems to match evolving African practice better. More reflection is needed on how such a concept might be integrated into the multilateralist framework of the ASF. There is a need for mechanisms to help mitigate against abuse by elites and strong powers.

Planning and adaptation of the ASF must take into account the fact that most AU missions are handed over to the UN within six to eighteen months, making harmonization of standards with the UN highly desirable. However, the differences between UN peace operations and AU stabilization missions do pose considerable challenges to such a harmonization project. To enable smoother transitions, the UN Security Council could consider funding a joint

AU–UN transition project consisting of training in UN peacekeeping doctrine, equipping forces according to UN standards, and upgrading their bases to UN standards, starting at least six months prior to the transfer of authority to a UN mission, or sooner, as was done in the CAR in 2014.

Although handover to the UN is the most plausible route, it is not guaranteed, so AU missions should therefore still be planned as distinct and comprehensive but as 'minimal' as possible. Most AU operations to date have created the conditions necessary for the UN to follow up with a multidimensional peacekeeping operation. That said, a transfer of authority to the UN must not become the overriding objective of the operation: the case-specific political objectives in themselves should be primary, and the AU mission must itself include the components and capabilities necessary for achieving them. Therefore, the political objective and peacebuilding process need to be considered at the planning stage, taking into account the vital role of civilians and police for longer-term stability and peacebuilding. However, as yet the AU cannot raise the internal resources it would need to deploy comprehensive multidimensional missions, and therefore AU missions have thus far deployed with modest numbers of police and civilian peacekeepers.

The principle of subsidiarity and the relationship between the UN, the AU and the RECs/RMs

As Ndiaye (Chapter 4) and others have described in this volume, the principle of subsidiarity lies at the heart of the debate on UN, AU, REC/RM relations, and resurfaces at regular intervals. Two fundamental principles are in tension when dealing with conflicts on the African continent – and elsewhere in the world. First, legal authority is drawn from the global to the local level, with the legal authority to use force residing with the UN Security Council. Secondly, ownership runs in the opposite direction from the local to the global level, with proximity being a decisive factor. These lines of authority, accountability and ownership follow each other closely, but are strengthened in opposite directions. At the intersection of these lines we find the African Union. The experience of the African Support Mission to Mali (AFISMA) highlighted many of the unresolved tensions and unclear divisions of roles between the UN, the AU and, in this case, the Economic Community of West Africa (ECOWAS). The transitions from MICOPAX, the mission of the Economic Community of Central African States (ECCAS), to the AU's African Support Mission in Central Africa Republic (MISCA) in December 2013, followed approximately six months later by the transition from MISCA to the UN Multidimensional Integrated Stabilization Mission in the CAR (MINUSCA), reflected some improvement and showed that the UN, the AU and the RECs can through consultations learn from previous experiences and adapt to new realities.

These experiences show that, when it comes to the authority to use non-consensual force,[1] all peace operations require authorization from the UN Security Council under Chapter VII of the UN Charter. The AFISMA experience further confirmed that the UN Security Council will no longer authorize an African REC/RM to undertake a peace operation, as with ECOMOG and ECOMIL in the past, without the consent and authority of the AU Peace and Security Council. All African peace operations to date have been undertaken by the African Union Commission, in close cooperation with the relevant REC/RMs and troop- and police-contributing countries. However, should a scenario arise where a REC/RM is called on to undertake a peace operation that requires the use of non-consensual force, authorization by the UN Security Council would be required. Practice as well as precedent indicate that the deployment of African peace operations will require the further authorization of the AU Peace and Security Council. If a REC/RM is mobilized to undertake such an operation, further authorization may be necessary from the REC/RM's own legal authorizing body.

In addition to the legal dimension, the principle of subsidiarity also has a practical dimension: the body nearest to the problem is likely to have the greatest practical and operational credibility and know-how to solve the problem. Thus, conflict management approaches in Africa will rely, in the first instance, on the advice, local knowledge and capacity of immediate neighbours, the regional body and the continental body. In some cases, owing to conflicts of interest or the distraction of other crises, the REC/RM may not be able to act as a first responder – but, as a general rule, the body closest to the problem will have responsibility for responding to an emerging crisis. If necessary, help can be sought from the next-highest authority, until eventually the assistance of the UN may be sought. In reality, in today's conflicts, the relevant REC, the AU and the UN are all likely to be present and to have prior existing engagements and commitments. However, whenever the question arises as to who should lead a particular initiative, and provided that it does not require legal authority to use force, the body nearest to the problem – the relevant REC/RM – should be assumed to have responsibility for responding first. That said, all the actors should coordinate closely with each other; and while the principle of subsidiarity should be a guide, it should not prevent the relevant REC/RM, the AU or the UN from choosing a different course of action, whether on the basis of comparative advantages, deployed capabilities or available resources.

Mission support

As Lotze (Chapter 6) highlighted, a well-functioning system for mission support is a critical factor for the success of peace operations, but continues to be the weakest and most neglected pillar of African peace operations. The difficult security environments in which African peace operations operate entail various challenges as regards mission support. Efforts are under way to further increase the support provided by AU member states for African peace operations, but it is also important to consider a more predictable international support system for regional operations. Globalization in this context implies that all conflicts have causes and effects linked to developments in the global system, and it is thus in the interests of the maintenance of global peace and security to find better and more predictable ways in which regional and international partners can work together in mandating and undertaking regional operations.

There has been insufficient investment in the planning and management of missions, in particular the support pillar. It is obviously difficult to plan for operations when the context is rapidly changing and there is little knowledge of what assets and capabilities will be available. Compounding these challenges, everything – from aviation and fuel to communications – has been dependent on the AU's partners, which is an obvious impediment to mission planning and execution. Greater capacity for mission support is needed at the level of the AU and the RECs/RMs. The AU should consider establishing a dedicated branch within its PSOD for this purpose. The UN has been improving its model for mission support and the AU and the UN should, *inter alia*, consider options for how the AU can access resources from the UN regional logistics bases in Brindisi and Entebbe. The AU should explore how it can cooperate with the UN on the development of strategic bases, tools, systems, stocks and outsourcing agreements.

On the ground, parallel standards exist for troops deployed by the UN and the AU in the same theatre. Reimbursement rates and support are provided according to the mission to which one belongs, not the country or situation to which one is deployed. The inequality of reimbursements also impacts on what member-state contributions are made available to what missions (AU versus UN). The lifespan of equipment decreases and maintenance costs increase because of the nature of the African peace operations. For example, in Somalia the budget for tyres for vehicles becomes exhausted as tyres are frequently rendered useless because of the prevalence, far beyond mission-planning assumptions, of improvised explosive devices (IEDs).

Contingent-owned equipment (COE) remains a significant challenge. Not all TCCs and PCCs have their own equipment, so one option would be to establish a pool of equipment that these can draw from. TCCs could be provided with loans to buy equipment delivered directly to the missions, for subsequent reimbursement. Only the USA and the NATO countries combined can undertake strategic airlifts, and commercial strategic airlifts are beyond the financial limits available to the AU or the UN. Commercial logistics are considerably more effective than the UN in combat situations, given the increasing risk aversion of the UN system.

To date, none of the designated support models is coherent with the type of high-intensity stabilization/peace enforcement missions that the AU is performing. Structured consultations are needed on this matter between the AU, the UN, the RECs and partners. Flexible models have been developed in response to specific contexts, reflecting continued ad hoc inventions here and now. At the AU, there has not been much incentive to draft sufficient support models, because of the reliance on external support. UNSOA, in support of AMISOM, is an advantageous model that can be further developed. In this security context there are advantages to having models that are 'lean and mean', with less staff working in an integrated manner with the AU. However, the UNSOA model could be improved by separating civilian from military personnel to a lesser degree. There should be joint efforts at better planning and implementing support solutions. Although the models that will be developed for future missions will also be significantly influenced by the political will of partners, the AU and the UN can identify what has worked and where improvements can be made.

Funding African peace operations

The funding of AU peace operations remains a critical concern. The June 2015 AU Summit decided that African states should take responsibility for at least 25 per cent of the cost of AU operations, but it was decided to gradually introduce this commitment over a period of five years. The 2015 High-level Independent Panel on Peace Operations supports the AU's call for more systematic and predictable financing models for UN-authorized AU-led peace operations, and encourages the use of trust funds and UN assessed contributions to fund African missions (UN 2015). If the AU decision is implemented it is likely to leverage more predictable support for AU-led operations from the UN and other strategic partners.

There is a need to further standardize and harmonize TCC and PCC contributions to African peace operations. This will enhance interoperability and facilitate support. The development of standards should not merely replicate standards for UN peacekeeping, but attempt innovative approaches that take into account the particular nature of African high-intensity peace operations.

Civilian and police dimensions of African peace operations

In her chapter, Akpasom (Chapter 8) detailed how multidimensionality remains critical to African peace operations, and the importance of articulating more clearly what the AU means by 'multidimensional' and what roles civilians and police can play. Military solutions should be used as a last resort – and even then they have their limitations in facilitating sustainable political outcomes or setting the stage for longer-term peacebuilding activities. All AU missions have military, police and civilian components under civilian leadership. However, the military dimension currently outweighs the others, in numbers as well as in importance, even though both the police and the civilian components are central for facilitating the transition to longer-term stability and mission exit.

The civilian dimensions of African peace operations have been slimmer than in UN missions owing to the high-intensity environment, among other reasons. Civilian functions thus tend to be gathered under broad headings – such as *Protection of Civilians*, which integrates perspectives on human rights, international humanitarian law, gender, sexual exploitation and abuse, and management of detainees; *Stabilization*, which integrates perspectives on security and governance, conflict management, quick impact projects and institution-building; and *Humanitarian Support*, which integrates issues related to civilian–military coordination, and security of internally displaced persons and refugees. All the same, the officers who conduct work in these areas are of paramount importance to the successful conclusion of the missions they support.

To increase the chances of mission success, civilians have been given an increased role in the planning elements of the AU. This is a positive trend that should be supported and reinforced. It is necessary to continue to develop the doctrinal framework and to impress upon African member states the significance of committing to accepted guidelines on key concepts such as protection of civilians, gender, humanitarian support, and combating sexual exploitation and abuse. The military dimension of stabilization missions has been overemphasized, to the detriment of a focus on political objectives, rule of law, police and civilian aspects. Planning must also reflect the various realities existing in parallel on the ground – one part of a country may enjoy relative stability while another could be embroiled in conflict.

Police support in stabilization contexts will necessarily provide distinct challenges that should be reflected in the doctrine, planning and conduct of policing tasks. African missions in high-intensity environments need formed police units (FPUs) equipped with armoured personnel carriers (APCs) to be relevant to the tasks of the mission. Police contributions should be deployed with the training they need, and training should focus on strengthening the capacity of the local police. It is also important to address the larger range of rule-of-law challenges, of which the police are only one part.

Further work is needed to provide the right people at the right time and at the right place. Guidance on training, rostering and recruitment needs has been developed, but more efforts are needed to generate appropriate staff on time. Finally, it is essential to consider what core civilian capabilities are needed in high-intensity situations, and what capacities could make the most impact. Political officers and human rights officers are obviously important – but also gender and conduct and discipline officers can help the mission to achieve its objectives, while also preventing and investigating misconduct and unwanted consequences.

From the Janjaweed to Boko Haram

As the subtitle of this book suggests, the AU peace operations experience developed from an initial focus on protecting civilians against the Janjaweed and other armed groups in Darfur, in an operation that did not rely on the use of force and that was essentially a defensive mandate, to its most recent mutation, where an AU-endorsed MNJTF of the Lake Chad Basin countries is engaged in offensive combat missions against Boko Haram. The AMIB and AMIS experiences were modelled on UN ceasefire and peace agreement missions, but the African experience has diverged significantly since then. The AU missions in especially Somalia, the CAR and against the Lord's Resistance Army, and its support for the MNJTF against Boko Haram, have developed into a new African stabilization model where offensive force is used to actively regain control over territory controlled by rebel groups, with the aim of weakening and eventually defeating those aggressors committed to violence, and to force their political associates to the negotiating table.

The ASF should remain the main framework of African peace operations. It will be important to actively work towards harmonizing the RDC and ACIRC concepts, to reflect further on the various mission scenarios most likely for the future deployment of African peace operations, and to focus on the specialized and niche capacities the AU and RECs/RMs need to develop or enhance. Most importantly, the experiences of the past decade suggest that the AU needs to retain a high great degree of flexibility so that it can continue to adapt to the highly dynamic and complex challenges it will be called upon to manage.

Note

1 In this context, the non-consensual use of force refers to those cases where the AU or a REC/RM is not requested by a state to intervene on its behalf. If a state requests another state or a regional body to assist in acting against an insurgency, no UN Security Council authority is needed, because the state is acting under its own sovereign authority. However, if the AU or a REC/RM should wish to mobilize and deploy a peace operation under the auspices of the ASF to respond to such a request, then it is conceivable that the PSC would need to authorize the use of the ASF.

References

African Union (2015) 'China donates USD1.2 million to support the AU Mission in Somalia', 8 September, www.peaceau.org/uploads/press-release-china-donates-8-9-15.pdf, accessed 18 November 2015.

Karlsrud, J. (2015) 'The UN at war: examining the consequences of peace enforcement mandates for the UN peacekeeping operations in the CAR, the DRC and Mali', *Third World Quarterly*, 36(1): 40–54.

Peen-Rodt, A. and J. Okeke (2013) 'AU–EU "Strategic Partnership": strengthening policy convergence and regime efficacy in African peace and security complex', *African Security*, 6(3/4): 211–33.

UN (United Nations) (2015) *Report of the High-level Independent Panel on United Nations Peace Operations: Uniting our Strengths for Peace*, 16 June, New York: United Nations, www.un.org/sg/pdf/HIPPO_Report_1_June_2015.pdf , accessed 18 November 2015.

About the contributors

Mustapha Abdallah (Ghana) is a research fellow in the Faculty of Academic Affairs and Research at the Kofi Annan International Peacekeeping Training Centre in Accra, Ghana.

Yvonne Akpasom (Uganda/South Africa) is the head of the Peace and Security Unit at the Deutsche Gesellschaft für Internationale Zusammenarbeit GmbH in Abuja, Nigeria. Prior to this, she was the African Union civilian adviser to the ECOWAS Commission from 2014 to 2015 and served also as a civilian planning and liaison officer at the Peace Support Operations Division of the African Union Commission in Addis Ababa, Ethiopia (2010–13).

Kwesi Aning (Ghana) is director of the Faculty of Academic Affairs and Research at the Kofi Annan International Peacekeeping Training Centre in Accra, Ghana. He serves as a professor of peacekeeping practice at Kennesaw State University, USA. Dr Aning also currently serves on the UN Secretary General's Advisory Board for the Peacebuilding Fund.

Linda Darkwa (Ghana) holds a PhD in human rights in political sciences from the Scuola Superiore Sant'Anna, in Pisa, Italy. She is currently a research fellow at the Legon Centre for International Affairs and Diplomacy at the University of Ghana, Legon.

Solomon A. Dersso (Ethiopia), a commissioner at the African Commission on Human and Peoples' Rights, is a legal scholar and analyst of African Union affairs and peace and security in Africa. A non-faculty professor of human rights at the College of Law and Governance at Addis Ababa University, Dr Dersso has led the work of the Institute for Security Studies on the African Union as head of the Peace and Security Council Report.

Walter Lotze (South Africa/Germany) is a senior researcher at the Centre for International Peace Operations, and an associate researcher with the Norwegian Institute of International Affairs. He previously worked with the African Union Mission in Somalia, the African Union Peace Support Operations Division and the African Centre for the Constructive Resolution of Disputes.

Michelle Ndiaye (Senegal) is director of the Africa Peace and Security Programme, African Union/Institute for Peace and Security Studies, Addis

Ababa University, Ethiopia, and head of secretariat of the Tana High-level Forum on Security in Africa. She consecutively headed several African and international organizations as managing director of the Mandela Institute for Development Studies, executive director of Greenpeace Africa and CEO of the African Institute for Corporate Citizenship.

Jide Martyns Okeke (Nigeria) is head of the Policy Development Unit within the Peace Support Operations Division of the African Union Commission in Addis Ababa, Ethiopia. He is concurrently a non-stipendiary visiting fellow at the University of Portsmouth, United Kingdom, with a research focus on peace and security in Africa (broadly defined) and Responsibility to Protect.

Index

Abdallah, Mustapha, 5, 92, 107
Abuja, 61
accountability, 117
Accra, Kotoka airport, 25
ACIRC (African Capacity for Immediate
Response to Crises) proposed, 4, 6,
11-12, 91, 101, 103, 116, 137, 144; concept
of, 16; creation decision 2013, 123;
establishment of, 103; 'gap-filling'
mechanism, 46; implications of, 106;
interim measure, 107; lead-nation
model, 129; operational concept for,
99; troop-contributing countries, 100;
Volunteering Nations, 99, 102
Addis Ababa, 97-8, 100-1, 125
AFISMA (African-led Support Mission
to Mali), 39, 42, 55, 59-61, 66, 81-3, 85,
108, 114, 122, 139, 140; African funding
of, 15; civilian component lack, 112;
stabilization responsibilities, 113
Africa Contingency Operations Training
Assistance (ACOTA), 103
Africa: contemporary peace operations,
79; crisis response renaissance, 90; ex-
colonial powers interference, 73; IDPs,
1; intra-state conflicts, 92; militarized
missions, 105; multilateral institutions,
21; peace and security architecture,
120; peace operations models, 80
'rising' narrative of, 17, 137; 'security
predicament', 21; UN authorized peace
operations, 71; water stress, 25
African Charter on Democracy, Elections
and Governance, 33
African Common Position on UN Peace
Operations, 124
African Mission in Burundi (AMIB), 80,
122, 144
African Peace Facility (APF), 84
African Peacekeeping Rapid Response
Partnership (APREP), 103
African Standby Capacity Roster, 110
Akpasom, Yvonne, 12, 15-16, 43, 49, 122,
129, 142

Al-Libi, Abu Anas, 24
Al-Qaddafi, Muammar, 29; ousting of, 24
Al-Qaeda, 27; in the Islamic Maghreb
(AQIM), 28; threats from, 22
Al-Shabaab, 42, 48, 58; areas recaptured
from, 113; dislodging campaign, 12;
East Africa, 23; Somalia, 28; sustained
influence, 92
Algeria, 55, 59, 100; Northern Sahel
power, 60
Amani Africa II, training exercise cycle,
96, 100, 137
Ametepe, Nayele (Ruby Adu-Gyamfi), 25
AMIS (African Union Mission in Sudan),
66, 83, 85, 144; budget limits, 13
AMISOM (African Union Mission in
Somalia), 12, 23, 39-40, 49, 56, 58, 66,
69, 71, 82-3, 85, 108, 112-13, 122, 128,
131, 136, 142; experience developed, 47;
insufficiency of, 43; mandate, 41; police
component, 42, 109, 114; UNSOA, 81
Angola, 100; ACIRC battalion pledged,
99
Aning, Kwesi, 5, 92, 107
Anna, Kofi, 55
Ansar al-Sharia, 24, 29
Ansar Dine, 23
APF (African Peace Facility), protection,
112; creation of, 53; emerging, 120;
external funding need consequences
funds capacity development, 85
APSA (African Peace and Security
Architecture), 3-4, 38-9, 52, 57, 63,
69, 91-2, 103, 107-8, 116, 136; ASF,
see below; civilians, 5; principles
consideration need, 16
Arab Spring, 29
armed groups: factionalized militant, 43;
traditional rebel decline, 44
ASF (African Standby Force of APSA),
10, 12, 17, 38-9, 44, 57, 94, 96, 110,
132, 144; -ACIRC Roadmap, 138;
adjustment need, 137; capacity-building
programmes, 97; civilian dimension,